FESTIVE OCCASIONS
~ COOKBOOK ~

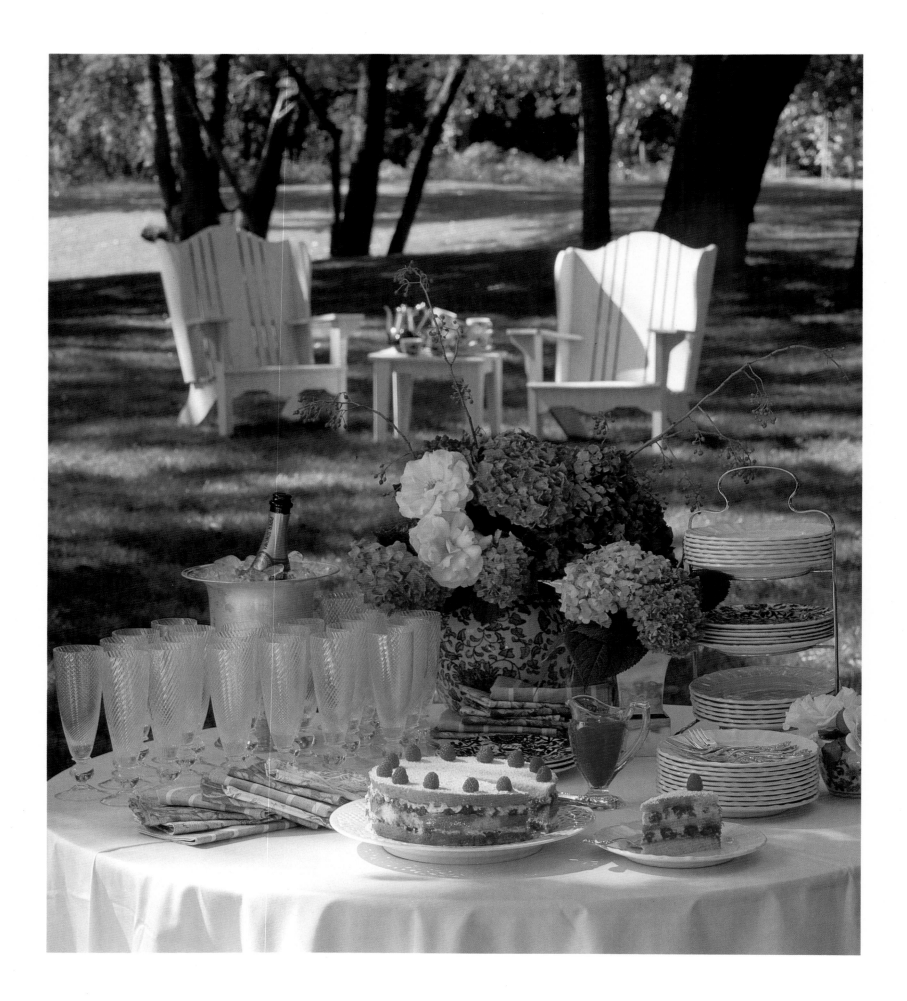

FESTIVE OCCASIONS
COOKBOOK

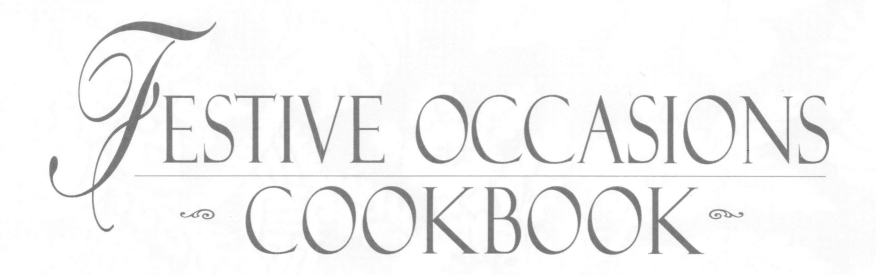

FESTIVE OCCASIONS COOKBOOK

GENERAL EDITOR

CHUCK WILLIAMS

MENU CONCEPTS & RECIPES

JOYCE GOLDSTEIN

PHOTOGRAPHY

ALLAN ROSENBERG & ALLEN V. LOTT

First Published in the U.S.A. in 1993 by
Weldon Owen Inc.
814 Montgomery Street
San Francisco, CA 94133

In collaboration with Williams-Sonoma
100 North Point, San Francisco, CA 94133

The Williams-Sonoma Entertaining Series
conceived and produced by Weldon Owen Inc.

WILLIAMS-SONOMA
Founder/Vice-Chairman: Chuck Williams

WELDON OWEN INC.
President: John Owen
Publisher: Wendely Harvey
Managing Editor: Tori Ritchie
Consulting Editor: Norman Kolpas
Copy Editor: Carolyn Miller
Editorial Assistant: Janique Poncelet
Design: John Bull, The Book Design Company
Design Assistant: Patty Hill
Production: Stephanie Sherman, Mick Bagnato,
 Jim Obata
Photography: Allan Rosenberg and Allen V. Lott
Additional Photography: Peter Johnson
Consulting Stylist: Sandra Griswold
Prop Stylist: Karen Nicks
Food Stylist: Susan Massey
Assistant Food Stylists: Heidi Gintner, Danielle Di Salvo
Additional Food Styling: Janice Baker
Wine Consultant: Evan Goldstein
Menu Illustrations: Gretchen Shields
Glossary Illustrations: Alice Harth

Library of Congress
Cataloging-in-Publication Data:

Festive occasions cookbook/general editor Chuck
  Williams, menu concepts & recipes Joyce Goldstein,
  photography Allan Rosenberg & Allen V. Lott.
        p.   cm. — (Williams-Sonoma entertaining series)
     Includes index.
     ISBN 1-875137-23-8
     1. Cookery, International. 2. Holiday cookery.
  3. Menus. I. Williams, Chuck. II. Goldstein, Joyce
  Esersky. III. Series.
  TX725.A1F435 1993
  641.5'68--dc20   93-12980
                                        CIP

Manufactured by Mandarin Offset, Hong Kong
Printed in Hong Kong

A Weldon Owen Production

A Note on Weights and Measures:
*All recipes include customary U.S., U.K. and metric
measurements. Conversions are based on a standard
developed for these books and have been rounded off.
Actual weights may vary.*

CONTENTS

INTRODUCTION

OCCASIONS

HOLIDAYS

ELEMENTS OF ENTERTAINING

$\mathcal{I}$NTRODUCTION

So many of life's moments, big and small, are worthy of special celebration: a traditional holiday, a birthday or anniversary, a homecoming. Any such occasion becomes even more festive when recognized with good food, lovingly prepared and served.

Think back to the most memorable parties you've ever given or attended and you'll probably discover that one word applies to them all: *effortless*. A truly festive occasion flows with a life and style all its own. Of course, magical though they seem, such events don't happen miraculously. From the first cause for celebration to the final cleanup, great parties result as much from organization as from creativity. This book aims to provide you with both. Whether you use it for a grand holiday feast or a simple welcome-home dinner, its goal is to make the event as easy and enjoyable for you, the host or hostess, as it is for your guests.

ENTERTAINING WITH STYLE

First and foremost, *Festive Occasions* can help take the fear out of entertaining. Like a personal party consultant, it guides you through the particulars of planning, leaving you free not only to add your own inimitable style, but also to enjoy the party as it happens. Every bit of information in this book is designed to help guide you while also inspiring you. The sixteen menus are divided into two sections, one for year-round celebrations, the other tailor-made for holidays. Each menu begins with all the practical information you will need to organize the meal, from preparation tips and decorating ideas to wine recommendations and strategies for cooking in advance. In most cases, the recipes have been written to yield six servings and can easily be multiplied for larger parties.

❧ The menus in *Festive Occasions* have been created and planned by master chef and cookbook author Joyce Goldstein. The recipes are geared not only to the occasion but to the time of year. Cooking methods are straightforward and much of the work can be done ahead. While all the dishes in each menu are crafted to work together, you can prepare as many or as few as suit your needs. Most of the recipes work for everyday cooking, too, in all sorts of combinations. And you'll probably find new favorites that will become permanent parts of your culinary repertoire.

❧ When you are ready to entertain, start with the planning strategies presented in this introduction.

To find a menu that suits your specific occasion or provides you with a fresh idea, choose from the table of contents. For step-by-step instructions on how to set a table, fold a napkin, arrange flowers and more, consult the "Elements of Entertaining" appendix at the back of the book (pages 174–185). For an explanation of cooking terms and special ingredients, consult the glossary beginning on page 186.

STRATEGIES FOR FESTIVE PARTIES

More than you may realize, the success of a party depends on the guest list. Though it may be stating the obvious, it is essential that your guests enjoy each other's company. To that end, give careful thought to the people you might invite. Consider their interests and personalities and try to select a dynamic blend.

❧ Think, too, about mixing guests in a way likely to encourage conversation. For a sit-down affair with a guest of honor, shuffle the seating between courses so that everyone gets a chance to sit near him or her. For cocktail parties, pay attention to the positioning of the food tables and bar area so that people can gather in comfortable spaces.

❧ To assist you in such deliberations, you might want to keep a party logbook, entering details of each occasion's guest list, seating, menu and other pertinent details. Refer back to it when planning future events and you'll soon gain a reputation as someone who entertains wisely and well.

EXTENDING AN INVITATION

In these busy times, it is important to invite guests well in advance. For an informal dinner, invitations should be extended at least a week ahead. More formal occasions, or parties for which you're inviting people you don't know as well, require the courtesy of at least two weeks' notice. Traditional holidays or gala events like a wedding, engagement or anniversary call for invitations at least one month ahead.

❧ The more formal the occasion, the more it merits printed or written invitations. Recommended formal etiquette calls for your name(s) and the words *request(s) the pleasure of your company,* followed by the occasion, date and time, suggested attire and the letters *RSVP*: an abbreviation of the French request for a response, *répondez s'il vous plaît.* Include your phone number beside or beneath the RSVP if a telephone response is acceptable.

❧ An invitation to a casual meal can be extended orally, but that leaves details open to confusion. A handwritten note, including date, time and an RSVP request, will provide your invitee with a more tangible, accurate reminder. If necessary, call a day or two before the party to confirm.

KEEPING IT RUNNING SMOOTHLY

Observe good hosts or hostesses in action and you'll see that no detail of their guests' comfort goes unnoticed. Becoming a great host or hostess is as easy as making a personal commitment to your guests.

❧ Make a mental checklist to refer to as the party progresses. Keep a constant eye out for guests' needs. If you see someone monopolizing a conversation, or another with no one to talk to, diplomatically mix up groups. Informal introductions performed by you, rather than by your guests, help break the ice, too.

❧ You may want to consider bringing in help, particularly for large or very formal gatherings. Word of mouth can lead you to reliable firms that supply caterers, wait staff, bartenders and others to share the work or do it all; you'll also find listings in the telephone directory (be sure to ask for and check references). Also consider asking friends or their teenage children, or your children's friends, to help out.

❧ Whatever happens, don't admit it when things go wrong and don't panic. Far more likely than not, a recipe you accidentally overcooked will not be noticed by your guests as long as you don't announce the mistake. Remember that a great party usually develops a life of its own, independent of your plans. Relax and enjoy it yourself and your guests will too.

DECIDING ON THE MENU, SELECTING THE WINES

The occasion itself is your first guide to the foods you might serve. Some holidays have their traditional dishes. Celebrations call for special ingredients and presentations, while less formal foods may be served at a casual gathering. Remember, though, that a few dishes well prepared and served are better than too many that are not well done.

❧ Whatever the occasion, consider which seasonal ingredients might be at their best. Review your guest list and records of past parties to make sure you'll cater to special tastes or dietary needs. And don't serve too much food; guests leave a table happier when satisfied rather than overfed.

❧ If time allows, you could prepare and serve at least part of the menu for a family meal a week or so before the party to practice. Such a dry run will familiarize you with the recipes and make it even easier to prepare them for the real event.

❧ Once you've selected the menu, the choice of accompanying wines becomes clearer. For every menu in this book, master sommelier Evan Goldstein has provided general wine guidelines and specific varietal suggestions. But some basic rules also bear repeating.

❧ Red with meat, white with fish is the oldest maxim in the canon of wine wisdom. But today the rule is flexible. Poultry, lighter meats like veal or pork, and richer seafood like salmon or lobster go well with either light red wines or robust whites. Sauces and garnishes also influence your choice, as does the number of courses.

❧ Despite these considerations, the decision need not be complicated. Start with the suggestions found with each menu. Then, seek out a knowledgeable local wine merchant to help you in your deliberations and pay strong attention to your personal preferences. Furthermore, don't feel that you have to pay a lot to ensure quality; good wine doesn't have to be expensive nowadays.

SHOPPING & COOKING AHEAD

The more cooking you can do beforehand, the lighter your workload and anxiety on the day of the party. Many of the recipes in this book lend themselves to advance preparation. Several days before your party, double-check your selected recipes along with the preparation list that appears with each menu. This way you'll know when to shop so that you have ingredients needing advance preparation (meat requiring marination, for example) on hand at the right moment.

❧ No matter the size of the party, the importance of list-making cannot be overemphasized. We recommend that you first read carefully through each recipe and prepare a master shopping list. Divide it into those things you can purchase at the supermarket and those that come from specialty food or wine shops. (You'll find that most of the ingredients in this book can be purchased at a good-quality food shop. It is helpful, too, to have access to a reliable butcher and fishmonger.) Check the list against your supplies, marking off the items that you already have. Also list which cooking utensils, pots, pans, baking dishes and so on are required and check that you have everything on hand. Make another list of flowers, candles, linens and any decorations you might need. Purchase, borrow or rent whatever is necessary to fill in the gaps.

SETTING THE SCENE

The dining room is the most obvious place to set a meal. But try thinking beyond those four walls. A casual party could be held happily in a spacious kitchen, family room or den. For a large, formal dinner, consider clearing an area in the living room for the table. An intimate dinner may call for a small table by the fireside or near a window.

When the weather allows, move the feast outdoors if possible.

❧ Don't forget to clean the house well in advance. Check the guest bathroom for sufficient hand towels, soap and other supplies. Designate an area for hanging coats, too; if the weather is inclement you don't want wet garments thrown on your bed.

Tables & Chairs

For a small party, your dining table and chairs will no doubt meet your needs. As the guest list increases, feel free to press tables and chairs from other rooms into service and use other surfaces as buffet counters. Consider rentals if you don't have enough furniture to meet your needs.

❧ Above all, anticipate your guests' comfort. Try sitting in every seat to make sure there is enough leg room and that chairs are at the right height; move chairs around and provide cushions if necessary.

Choosing Tableware

Your selection of tableware will play an important role in setting a style for the party. Ideally, dishware should flatter the food you are serving and play to any theme you might have (such as Italian ceramics

for a Mediterranean menu). On a more practical level, however, you need to work with what's available, so count to be sure you have enough pieces for the menu you've selected and for the number of guests. Don't hesitate to mix and match patterns. If you need rentals, call at least a week ahead. Or consider borrowing dishes from a friend.

Flowers & Other Centerpieces

Well-planned centerpieces enhance a party's festive air. Flowers are the most obvious choice, but all kinds of items can be incorporated, such as shells, ribbons, twigs and leaves. Beautifully arranged seasonal vegetables, fruits or herbs also make stunning non-floral decorations.

❧ You'll find step-by-step hints on pages 184 and 185, as well as ideas with every menu in this book, for centerpieces from plain to fancy. Always bear in mind that the best ones are low and spread out, allowing guests to see each other across the table.

Lighting & Music

A night or two before an evening party, turn on all the lights and look over the setting. If you can, reposition lamps to help define conversation areas.

❧ Candlelight always adds to the ambience and flatters anyone seen in its glow. But be sure to use supplementary electric lights, or the room is likely to be too dark. It's best to use good-quality drip-free candles such as beeswax. Avoid scented candles, which can detract from the food and wine.

❧ Any music you select should serve to subtly enhance the mood. Your personal tastes will certainly play a part in the music you choose, but bear in mind guests' inclinations as well. For a very special occasion, you might want to employ musicians or a band. Always keep music low enough that it doesn't compete with normal conversational levels.

Gifts & Favors

Special events become all the more lasting when guests are offered mementos to take home. Whether it is a jar of homemade preserves, a bottle of wine with a personalized label, or even a small framed instant photograph used as a placecard, remember that a host gift should not be so grand that it causes embarrassment, requires a special effort of acknowledgment or makes guests feel obliged to reciprocate. Throughout this book, you'll find suggestions for host gifts that you may find useful or inspiring; use them as you see fit.

Putting It All Together

The main elements for a successful party generate from you: the guests, the setting, the accoutrements and the food. This book is designed to help you put them together with confidence and to be an all-encompassing resource for you to rely on. Every piece of information should be treated as a helpful suggestion as there is no such thing as a hard and fast rule for entertaining. In the end, we hope you'll use our ideas as inspiration to create a festive occasion that's entirely your own.

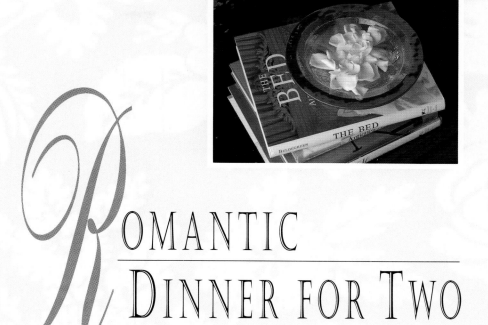

ROMANTIC
DINNER FOR TWO

WHETHER YOU ARE MARKING Valentine's Day, a special anniversary or some other shared occasion, celebrate with this memorable menu for two. We show it served at a fireside table where the warmth and glow of the flames enhance the mood of romance, but it could just as well be set in a cozy window alcove, on a balcony with a view or by candlelight at the kitchen table.

For this intimate meal, we chose china with a whimsical gold pattern and favorite pieces of silver. Heart-shaped accessories play up the amorous theme, from vases to napkin rings to the salsa ramekin. White flowers such as tulips or roses are simple, yet elegant, and are easy to arrange. Candlelight adds atmosphere as well; a tray of votives fits the scale of a table for two. You could also set small candles in various spots around the room.

A color scheme of white and gold, with heart-shaped accents, creates a very romantic place setting.

SURPRISINGLY, a dinner for two often entails more advance planning than a larger party. Try to complete most of the preparation ahead of time so you are free to devote the maximum attention to your dinner guest once the evening begins. You can marinate the squabs and make the dessert the night before, then boil the lobster the next day. Check the preparation list on the facing page to help you plan.

If your schedule is tight, serve fewer courses: oysters followed by lobster, or the pear salad followed by the squab. If you are opening the oysters yourself, be sure to do this just before dressing up to avoid splattering your clothes.

Menu

Casually arranged in a crystal vase on a side table, the delicate white blossoms and curving stems of tulips add to the ambience.

Oysters with Tangerine Salsa

❧

*Roast Lobster
with Meyer Lemon Butter*

❧

Broiled Squabs in Honey Marinade

Wild Rice

Pear, Fennel & Frisée Salad

❧

*Chocolate Pots de Crème
with Candied Rose Petals*

PREPARATION LIST

◆ The night before, marinate the squabs; make and refrigerate the pots de crème.

◆ In the morning, boil the lobster, remove and cut up the meat, refill the shells and chill; make and refrigerate the lemon butter.

◆ Several hours before dining, make the salsa.

◆ About 30 minutes before, start cooking the wild rice; remove the lemon butter and lobster from the refrigerator. Assemble the salad.

◆ Before dining, preheat the oven for the lobster; take the dessert from the refrigerator.

◆ While eating the oysters, roast the lobster.

◆ While eating the lobster, preheat the broiler for the squabs; dress the salad.

EACH RECIPE YIELDS 2 SERVINGS.

*A tray of votive candles illuminates a side table
on which an intriguing present awaits opening.*

WINE RECOMMENDATIONS

Start the evening with a high-quality, lighter-style California sparkling wine or a French Champagne. Continue it with the lobster, or go on to a half-bottle of classic Chardonnay or Sauvignon Blanc, or even a soft Pinot Noir. With the squab, serve a distinctive red wine such as Merlot or Côtes du Rhône. With dessert, pour generous snifters of your favorite brandy.

OYSTERS WITH TANGERINE SALSA

SERVES 2

You can use more or less jalapeño to taste in this sweet, tart, spicy salsa; but don't make it so hot that it dominates the oysters' flavor. To shuck the shellfish, you need an oyster knife (available at a well-stocked cookware store), or have your fishmonger shuck the oysters and pack them to go on the half shell.

1 small jalapeño (hot green) chili
   pepper, seeded and minced
grated zest and juice of 1 tangerine
freshly ground pepper to taste
12 oysters in the shell
rock salt

Combine the jalapeño, tangerine zest and juice. Add the pepper. Pour into a small ramekin or bowl.

☙ To open the oysters, hold each one in a heavy dish towel with the rounded side of the shell down. Work the tip of an oyster knife into the hinge near the narrow end of the shell; twist the knife to pop open the shell. Slide the knife along the inside of the upper shell to sever the muscle, then pull off the top shell and discard. Loosen the oyster from the bottom shell by sliding the knife under the oyster. Remove any bits of shell debris or sand.

☙ Spread some rock salt in a layer on a serving plate. Place the oysters in their shells on the plate and serve with the salsa. Spoon the salsa over the oysters to eat.

Oysters with Tangerine Salsa

ROAST LOBSTER WITH MEYER LEMON BUTTER

SERVES 2

If you can't find Meyer lemons, mix regular lemon juice and orange juice.

2 teaspoons minced shallot
2 teaspoons finely chopped
   fresh tarragon
2 tablespoons tarragon white
   wine vinegar
½ teaspoon grated Meyer lemon zest
   or regular lemon zest
1 tablespoon fresh Meyer lemon juice
   or 2 teaspoons fresh regular lemon
   juice plus 1 teaspoon orange juice

¼ cup (2 oz/60 g) unsalted butter
   at room temperature
salt and freshly ground pepper to taste
1 live Atlantic (Maine) lobster,
   about 1½ lb (750 g)

Place the shallot, tarragon and vinegar in a small saucepan and cook over high heat to reduce until the liquid is almost totally evaporated and syrupy. Stir in the lemon zest and juice. Let cool, then beat this mixture into the butter. Season to taste with salt and pepper. The butter may be made ahead and refrigerated, covered, up to 1 day.

☙ Bring a large pot of salted water to a boil, drop in the lobster and cook, covered, for 7–8 minutes. Plunge the lobster into cold water. Cut the lobster in half lengthwise and remove the meat from the body and claws as directed on page 188; clean and reserve the body shell halves. Cut all the lobster meat into bite-sized pieces and replace it in the body shell halves. Cover tightly and refrigerate up to 8 hours.

☙ To roast, let the lobsters and the lemon butter come to room temperature; preheat an oven to 350°F (180°C). Spread the butter over the lobster meat, cover loosely with aluminum foil and bake until heated through, about 8 minutes. Serve at once.

Roast Lobster with Meyer Lemon Butter

BROILED SQUABS IN HONEY MARINADE

SERVES 2

The marinade adds delicate flavor and helps the skin turn a burnished mahogany when cooked. Eat rare for the best flavor.

2 squabs, about 1 lb (500 g) each
1 star anise
2 whole cloves
seeds from 1 cardamom pod
one 2-inch (5-cm) piece fresh ginger, smashed with the side of a knife
⅔ cup (5 fl oz/160 ml) light soy sauce
⅓ cup (3 fl oz/90 ml) Scotch or bourbon
⅓ cup (4 oz/125 g) honey
salt, freshly ground pepper, ground ginger and ground cinnamon to taste

To prepare the squabs, insert a sharp knife through the neck cavity of each bird and cut through the back, leaving the breast intact. Remove the backbone, breastbone, cartilage and ribs. Cut the birds in half through the breast. Place the squabs in a glass or plastic container.
❧ Combine the star anise, cloves, cardamom seeds, fresh ginger and soy sauce in a small saucepan over moderate heat. Simmer for 5 minutes, remove from the heat and let steep for 30 minutes. Strain, reserving the liquid. Stir the Scotch or bourbon and honey into the liquid. Pour over the squabs, cover and refrigerate overnight, turning once.
❧ To cook, let the squabs come to room temperature. Preheat a broiler (griller). Lightly sprinkle the squabs with salt, pepper, ground ginger and ground cinnamon. Broil skin-side down for 3–4 minutes, then turn and broil 3–4 minutes on the other side for rare, or cook slightly longer if desired.

WILD RICE

SERVES 2

The nutlike taste of wild rice is the perfect foil for the sweetly marinated squab.

1½ cups (12 fl oz/375 ml) water
salt to taste
½ cup (3 oz/90 g) wild rice
2 tablespoons minced green part of a green (spring) onion
¼ cup (1 oz/30 g) toasted sliced almonds (see glossary)

In a medium saucepan, bring the water to a boil, add the salt and wild rice and reduce heat to a simmer. Cover and cook the wild rice until tender, about 1 hour.
❧ Stir in the green onion. Spoon the wild rice onto individual plates and garnish with the sliced almonds.

What could be more romantic than love letters? Perhaps this is the night to pull out those treasured reminders and read them again together.

PEAR, FENNEL & FRISÉE SALAD

SERVES 2

Served on the same plate as the squab and wild rice, this simple salad also could be served as a first course.

1 firm ripe Comice or other winter pear
1 small fennel bulb
1 small head frisée or 1 bunch watercress
¼ cup (2 fl oz/60 ml) white wine vinegar
2 teaspoons grated fresh ginger
½ teaspoon sugar
½ cup (4 fl oz/125 ml) olive oil
salt and freshly ground pepper to taste

Cut the pear in half lengthwise, remove the stem, core and seeds, then slice thin. Remove the tubular stems from the fennel, reserving any attractive fronds for a garnish, if you like. Cut the bulb into quarters lengthwise and remove the hard center core and any discolored outer portions. Slice thin. Trim the tough stems from the frisée or the watercress.
❧ In a small bowl, stir together the vinegar and grated ginger. Let stand for 5 minutes, then whisk in the sugar and the oil. Season with salt and pepper. Toss the frisée or watercress with half of the vinaigrette and divide between 2 plates. Arrange the pear and fennel slices over the greens and drizzle the rest of the vinaigrette on top. Garnish with the reserved fennel fronds, if using.

Broiled Squabs in Honey Marinade; Wild Rice; Pear, Fennel & Frisée Salad

CHOCOLATE POTS DE CRÈME WITH CANDIED ROSE PETALS

SERVES 2

You can find candied rose petals in gourmet shops, but making your own is quite easy. Be sure to use only unsprayed roses.

FOR THE POTS DE CRÈME:
⅔ cup (5 fl oz/160 ml) heavy
   (double) cream
2 oz (60 g) bittersweet chocolate, grated
2 teaspoons light brown sugar, packed
pinch of salt
2 egg yolks
½ teaspoon vanilla extract (essence)

FOR THE CANDIED ROSE PETALS:
unsprayed rose petals
1 egg white, lightly beaten
½ cup (4 oz/125 g) superfine
   (caster) sugar

To make the pots de crème, place the cream, chocolate, sugar and salt in the top of a double boiler and cook until scalding. Whisk the egg yolks lightly in a small bowl, then whisk in a bit of the hot chocolate cream to warm them. Gradually stir this mixture back into the cream in the double boiler and cook, stirring, over simmering water until thickened, about 10 minutes.

❧ Remove from the heat, stir in the vanilla and pour into pot de crème cups or small custard cups. Let cool uncovered, then chill until cold, about 2 hours or overnight. Remove from the refrigerator about 30 minutes before serving.

❧ Meanwhile, to make the candied rose petals, gently brush each flower petal with egg white, then sprinkle it with sugar. Place the petals on a cake rack and let dry, then use them to garnish the pots de crème.

After dinner, retire to a comfy spot and toast each other with a final sip of brandy. Generously sized snifters are perfect for swirling the spirit to develop its aroma. If you are fond of the best, look for Cognac, the classic French brandy. It's labeled according to its age, with the oldest (those that are aged more than 6½ years) bearing the X.O. designation. Each brand has its own characteristics that result from the blender's art.

Chocolate Pots de Crème with Candied Rose Petals

RITE-OF-SPRING BRUNCH

As DAYS GROW LONGER and warmer, the advent of spring brings with it a desire to celebrate. This is a good time to enjoy some of nature's finest produce with family and friends at a weekend party. Mother's Day, Easter or any other special event is a good reason for a rite-of-spring brunch.

The season suggests a fresh, simple decorative approach, so we selected dishware in pastel colors for this festive table. For a no-fuss centerpiece, we filled an assortment of clear glass vases and colored mineral-water bottles with colorful blossoms such as tulips, jonquils, Gerbera daisies and anemones. To take advantage of the morning light, this brunch could be set in a sun room or patio, or beside a window with a garden view. If the weather is warm, you might want to move the party outdoors.

THE BRUNCH MENU that follows features ingredients that reflect a blend of seasons: spring's tender young asparagus and peas, late-winter pears and last summer's preserved vine-ripened tomatoes. Each dish is easily prepared and presented, suiting the relaxed pace of a Saturday or Sunday morning.

The best strategy for a weekend meal is to serve it with a minimum of effort. For that reason, we set the table casually, letting guests help themselves to the first-course salad from a platter placed on a side table. Freshly cooked spaghetti may be presented on individual warm plates, with the asparagus and toasts passed alongside. Dessert also may be offered buffet-style, along with coffee and tea.

Menu

Pastel-colored plates highlight the tones of the salad. The folded napkins are rolled like scrolls so that their pointed ends echo the star-shaped napkin rings.

WINE RECOMMENDATIONS

With the salad, offer a light-bodied, herbaceous white wine: Sauvignon Blanc or Riesling. For the spaghetti, pour a medium-bodied Italian Chianti or, from California, a slightly peppery Zinfandel. For dessert, try an Italian Vin Santo or sweet Marsala.

Avocado, Grapefruit & Endive Salad

&

*Toast with
Sun-dried Tomato Purée*

*Spaghetti alla Carbonara
with Peas*

*Asparagus with
Toasted Almonds & Balsamic Vinaigrette*

&

Polenta Pound Cake

Red Wine–poached Pears

*Handwritten postcards double as clever invitations
and serve to remind guests of the exact date and time.*

PREPARATION LIST

◆ Up to 2 days before, prepare the sun-dried tomato purée; poach the pears.

◆ The day before, make the pound cake.

◆ The night before, prepare the grapefruit segments and vinaigrette for the salad.

◆ About 2 hours ahead, dice the pancetta and blanch the peas for the spaghetti.

◆ Up to 1 hour before eating, prepare the asparagus; boil the water for the spaghetti.

◆ Just before serving, cook the spaghetti; assemble and dress the salad.

EACH RECIPE YIELDS 6 SERVINGS.

Small glass vases bring blossoms close to each place setting.

AVOCADO, GRAPEFRUIT & ENDIVE SALAD

SERVES 6

Have this simple, refreshing salad ready and waiting to be served to guests as they are seated.

FOR THE VINAIGRETTE:

¼ cup (⅜ oz/10 g) chopped fresh
   mint, lightly packed
¼ cup (2 fl oz/60 ml) fresh
   lemon juice
½ cup (4 fl oz/125 ml) fresh grapefruit juice
1 cup (8 fl oz/250 ml) olive oil
3 tablespoons honey
1 tablespoon grated grapefruit zest
salt and freshly ground pepper to taste

FOR THE SALAD:

3 ripe avocados
3 pink grapefruits
4 small heads Belgian endive
   (chicory/witloof)
1 cup (1½ oz/40 g) fresh whole
   mint leaves
¼ cup (⅜ oz/10 g) chopped fresh mint

To make the vinaigrette, place the chopped mint and lemon juice in a small saucepan and bring to a boil. Remove from the heat and let steep for 10 minutes. Strain into a medium bowl. Add the grapefruit juice, olive oil, honey and zest and whisk together. Season with salt and pepper and adjust the sweet and tart ratio.

To make the salad, cut the avocados in half, remove the pit, scoop from the shell with a large spoon and cut into long, thin slices. Peel the grapefruits, remove all the white pith and cut between the membranes to release the

Avocado, Grapefruit & Endive Salad

grapefruit segments. Trim the ends from the endive and separate the leaves. Thinly slice the endive leaves lengthwise. ❧ Combine the endive and mint leaves in a salad bowl and dress with half the vinaigrette. Place on a serving platter or divide among 6 individual plates. Alternate the grapefruit segments and avocado slices atop the greens. Drizzle with the remaining vinaigrette and top with the chopped mint.

TOAST WITH SUN-DRIED TOMATO PURÉE

SERVES 6

Sun-drying is a traditional Italian way to preserve tomatoes. Spread this classic purée on slices of the best-quality bread you can make or buy.

1 cup (6 oz/185 g) oil-packed
   sun-dried tomatoes
1–2 cloves garlic, minced
½ cup (2½ oz/75 g) pitted
   black olives, such as Kalamata
olive oil as needed
½ cup (¾ oz/20 g) chopped fresh
   basil leaves, lightly packed
1 small baguette, sliced, or 12 slices
   fine-grained white bread, halved

*P*lace some of the oil from the sun-dried tomatoes in a small saucepan. Warm the minced garlic in this oil over medium heat for about 2 minutes to remove the bite. Combine the tomatoes, olives, garlic and a little olive oil in a food processor or blender. Pulse to combine to a smooth paste. Stir in the basil. Transfer the purée to a small bowl. Cover and store purée in the refrigerator for up to 2 days. ❧ Toast the bread slices. Spread with purée and serve, or offer the toasts in a basket with the purée alongside.

SPAGHETTI ALLA CARBONARA WITH PEAS

SERVES 6

Sauced with eggs, bacon and cheese, this classic Roman "charcoal-maker's" pasta is a fitting brunch dish. Fresh peas add a touch of spring.

¾ lb (375 g) lean pancetta or bacon
2 cups (8 oz/250 g) fresh shelled peas or
   thawed frozen peas
4 eggs
½ cup (2 oz/60 g) freshly grated
   Parmesan cheese or half pecorino
   romano and half Parmesan cheese
1 tablespoon freshly ground pepper
1 tablespoon salt
1 lb (500 g) spaghetti
2 tablespoons olive oil
additional grated Parmesan cheese and
   freshly ground pepper, optional

*U*nroll the pancetta and cut it crosswise into ¼-inch-wide (6-mm) strips; set aside. Blanch the peas in boiling salted water until tender-firm, about 1–2 minutes. Plunge into cold water, then drain and set aside. Beat together the eggs, cheese and pepper in a large serving bowl. Keep in a warm place near the stove or on a warming shelf. ❧ Bring a large pot of water to a boil. Add the salt, drop in the pasta and cook until al dente, 7–9 minutes. ❧ Meanwhile, heat the oil in a large sauté pan and add the pancetta. Cook, stirring occasionally, until the pancetta is cooked but not crisp, about 5 minutes. Set aside. ❧ When the pasta is al dente, drop the peas into the pasta pot to heat them through quickly. Drain the pasta and peas, add them to the bowl with the eggs, then add the pancetta and most of the drippings. Toss very quickly to combine. The sauce should be a thick liquid. Serve at once. Pass additional cheese and pepper if desired.

Spaghetti alla Carbonara with Peas; Toast with Sun-dried Tomato Purée

ASPARAGUS WITH TOASTED ALMONDS & BALSAMIC VINAIGRETTE

SERVES 6

You can serve the asparagus either hot or at room temperature, allowing you flexibility in make-ahead preparations.

2 lb (1 kg) fresh asparagus
¼ cup (2 oz/60 g) unsalted butter
¼ cup (2 fl oz/60 ml) olive oil
¾ cup (3 oz/90 g) toasted slivered
   almonds or pine nuts (see glossary)
⅓ cup (3 fl oz/90 ml) balsamic vinegar
   or to taste
salt and freshly ground pepper to taste

*T*rim the asparagus stalks to the same length. Bring about 2 inches (5 cm) salted water to a boil in a large frying pan; lay the asparagus in the pan and cook, uncovered, until tender-crisp, 3–5 minutes. Remove asparagus and plunge them into cold water, then drain and pat dry. Let cool to room temperature, then prepare the vinaigrette, or prepare the vinaigrette and serve at once.

❧ To prepare the vinaigrette, heat the butter and oil in a large sauté pan. Add the nuts and stir until hot. Add the balsamic vinegar and, when bubbly, pour over the asparagus. Season with salt and pepper and serve.

POLENTA POUND CAKE

MAKES ONE 9- BY 5- BY 3-INCH
(23- BY 13- BY 7.5-CM) LOAF

During baking, this dense loaf cake fills the kitchen with the sweet smell of corn. If you make it in advance, wrap it well in plastic until ready to serve.

1¼ cups (6 oz/185 g) all-purpose
   (plain) flour
2 teaspoons baking powder
½ teaspoon salt
¼ teaspoon ground nutmeg
1 cup (8 oz/250 g) unsalted butter at
   room temperature
1 cup (8 oz/250 g) sugar
6 eggs
1 teaspoon vanilla extract (essence)
½ teaspoon almond extract (essence)
grated zest of 1 lemon
¾ cup (4 oz/125 g) sifted yellow
   cornmeal

*B*utter and flour a 9- by 5- by 3-inch (23- by 13- by 7.5-cm) loaf pan. Preheat an oven to 350°F (180°C).

❧ Sift the flour, baking powder, salt and nutmeg together; set aside. In a large bowl, beat the butter and sugar together until fluffy. Add the eggs, vanilla, almond extract and lemon zest; beat well. Stir in the flour mixture and the cornmeal and combine well.

❧ Pour into the prepared loaf pan and bake until a toothpick inserted in the center of the loaf comes out clean, about 1 hour. Let cool in the pan for 15 minutes, then unmold onto a rack to finish cooling. Serve sliced.

*Asparagus with Toasted Almonds
& Balsamic Vinaigrette*

Polenta Pound Cake; Red Wine-poached Pears

RED WINE-POACHED PEARS

SERVES 6

Excellent with polenta pound cake, these are also good on their own, topped with whipped cream or zabaglione. Try the recipe with apples, too.

6 small, firm-ripe Bosc, Winter Nellis
   or Bartlett pears
juice of 1 lemon
grated zest of 1 lemon and 1 orange
1 cinnamon stick
1 star anise
3 whole cloves
1 cup (8 oz/250 g) sugar
½ cup (4 fl oz/125 ml) water
3 cups (24 fl oz/750 ml) dry red wine

Peel the pears and remove the cores from the bottom with a corer, or cut them in half and remove the cores. Set the pears aside in a bowl of water (to cover) mixed with the lemon juice until ready to use.

In a large saucepan or pot, stir together the grated zests, cinnamon, star anise, cloves, sugar, water and wine; bring to a boil. Add the pears, reduce heat to a simmer and poach, uncovered, until a skewer penetrates a pear easily, about 35 minutes for whole pears, 25 minutes for halves. Transfer the pears to a bowl with a slotted spoon. Let the poaching liquid cool, then pour it over the pears. Refrigerate overnight, or up to 2 days. Bring to room temperature, or warm slightly, before serving.

On a side table, a coffee and tea service is framed by casual bouquets of tulips.

$\mathcal{G}$ALA BUFFET

O N A WARM SPRING OR SUMMER DAY, what could be better than a sunny setting for celebrating an engagement, wedding, anniversary or graduation? A lawn, garden, patio or one or more bright rooms provides ample space for a large-scale gathering. For any of these important occasions, the food, decorations and setting should be both elegant and welcoming. To achieve this, we show one long rented table for seating guests, although of course you could seat guests at two or more smaller tables. For china, we selected blue and white heirloom plates. Flowers may be placed everywhere, in containers of all shapes and sizes.

To make an unforgettable place card, use an instant camera to snap photos of guests as they arrive, slipping the pictures into frames and placing them at each setting. At the party's end, they become charming keepsakes of the event.

Use an instant photo for a place card that's also a keepsake.

Menu

WITH THIS PARTY for twenty four, a buffet allows guests a greater opportunity to mingle. It is also the most logical way to serve a maximum number of people with minimal effort. The variety of recipes guarantees that there will be something to suit each person's taste. But you could prepare fewer dishes for a smaller gathering, or add recipes from other menus in this book for a larger group.

To make sure that all the buffet items are ready to serve at the same time, read through the preparation list and recipe introductions well ahead of the party. A caterer, friend or family member could provide help if your time is limited, but since all the food is served at room temperature, this menu is not difficult to assemble in advance.

Experiment with a variety of containers for your flowers: bowls, champagne buckets, silver teapots, egg cups, Chinese teacups and porcelain tumblers all stand in as vases.

Cheese Platter

❧

Shrimp with Oregano & Garlic

Celery, Mushroom & Endive Salad

*Fillet of Beef with Paprika,
Coriander & Cumin*

Rice & Wild Rice Salad

Tuna with Peppers & Olives

❧

Berry Tiramisù

PREPARATION LIST

◆ Four days ahead, start marinating the beef.

◆ The day before, sprinkle the beef with salt.

◆ The night before, prepare the tiramisù.

◆ Up to 4 hours ahead, make the rice salad.

◆ Three hours before, prepare the tuna.

◆ Up to 2 hours before, marinate the shrimp;
make the celery salad.

◆ One hour before, grill the shrimp and
roast the beef fillet.

EACH RECIPE YIELDS 6 OR MORE REGULAR-
SIZE SERVINGS. FOR A BUFFET PARTY FOR 24
GUESTS, AS SHOWN, MULTIPLY EACH RECIPE BY
THE QUANTITY INDICATED.

*Set up a liquor bar where guests can serve themselves; a
separate bar for wine and water could be set up on the lawn.*

WINE RECOMMENDATIONS

Offer both white and red wines. Choose
a medium-bodied white with fresh green
flavors, such as a light Chardonnay or a
French Chablis; for the red, try a Pinot Noir
or a Cabernet Sauvignon. With the tiramisù,
pour sparkling wine flavored with a little
berry liqueur or crème de cassis if desired.

Shrimp with Oregano & Garlic

SERVES 6 (MULTIPLY BY 2 FOR BUFFET)

Classic paella-style flavorings season these grilled shrimp. Make extra marinade to offer as a sauce, or simply garnish with lemon. If using wooden skewers, soak them first in warm water for 20 minutes.

36 large shrimp (prawns)
3 tablespoons dried oregano
1 tablespoon minced garlic
1 cup (8 fl oz/250 ml) olive oil
⅓ cup (3 fl oz/90 ml) sherry vinegar
salt and freshly ground pepper to taste
lemon wedges

Shell and devein the shrimp (see glossary); set aside. Warm the oregano and garlic in a small saucepan over medium heat with about 2 tablespoons of the olive oil for about 2 minutes to remove the bite. Remove from the heat and stir in the vinegar and the remaining oil. Season with salt and pepper. Let cool, then pour over the shrimp and marinate for up to 2 hours in the refrigerator.

❧ Prepare a fire in a grill. Position the oiled grill rack 4–6 inches (10–15 cm) above the fire. Or, preheat a broiler (griller). Lift the shrimp from the marinade and thread 3 shrimp on each of 12 skewers. Grill over hot coals or broil until pink, about 2 minutes on each side. Serve with lemon wedges.

Celery, Mushroom & Endive Salad

SERVES 6 (MULTIPLY BY 2 FOR BUFFET)

A piquant dressing complements the endive's mild bitterness. The dressed salad stays crisp for up to 2 hours.

½ cup (4 fl oz/125 ml) olive oil
¼ cup (2 fl oz/60 ml) toasted walnut oil
¼ cup (2 fl oz/60 ml) fresh lemon juice
¼ cup (2 fl oz/60 ml) heavy (double) cream
2 teaspoons Dijon mustard
salt and freshly ground pepper to taste
2 cups (8 oz/250 g) thinly sliced celery
½ lb (250 g) fresh mushrooms, thinly sliced
5 oz (155 g) Gruyère cheese, cut into long, thin strips
1 cup (4 oz/125 g) walnuts, toasted and coarsely chopped (see glossary)
3–4 heads Belgian endive (chicory/ witloof)

In a small bowl, whisk together the olive oil, walnut oil, lemon juice, cream and mustard until smooth. Season with salt and pepper.

❧ Combine the celery, mushrooms, cheese and walnuts in a large bowl. Add the vinaigrette and toss. Trim the ends from the endive and separate the leaves. Line a large platter with the endive leaves and top with the celery mixture. Or, pour the vinaigrette over the celery, mushrooms and cheese, toss well and use this mixture to fill the endive leaves. Place the filled leaves on a platter and top them with the chopped walnuts.

As an hors d'oeuvre, present a variety of cheeses, breads and crackers. Balance flavors and textures by offering creamy, hard and fresh cheeses such as (clockwise from top right): double-cream Brie, layered Gorgonzola and Cheddar, peppered goat cheese, dry jack, and two varieties of Port Salut. For easy service, place the cheese board near your wine bar.

Shrimp with Oregano & Garlic; Celery, Mushroom & Endive Salad

FILLET OF BEEF WITH PAPRIKA, CORIANDER & CUMIN

SERVES 6 (MULTIPLY BY 2 FOR BUFFET)

The beef, which gets an aromatic flavor from the spice rub, requires 4 days of marination. Serve it rare, leaving the end slices for those who like their meat well done.

1 fillet of beef, about 3½ lb (1.75 kg)

3 tablespoons paprika

2 teaspoons ground cumin

1 tablespoon ground coriander

2 tablespoons freshly ground pepper

1 teaspoon ground nutmeg

¼ teaspoon cayenne pepper

1 tablespoon salt

hot-sweet mustard

Trim the fillet of any visible fat and silverskin. Mix together the paprika, cumin, coriander, ground pepper, nutmeg and cayenne. Spread this spice mixture evenly over the beef. Place the meat in a large glass or plastic dish and cover. Let sit in the refrigerator for 4 days. On the third day, sprinkle the meat with the salt.

Tuna with Peppers & Olives; Fillet of Beef with Paprika, Coriander & Cumin; Rice & Wild Rice Salad

To cook, let the meat sit at room temperature for about 1 hour. Preheat a stove-top griddle or a large cast-iron frying pan and preheat an oven to 350°F (180°C). Sear the fillet on the griddle, or in the pan, until brown on all sides, about 6–8 minutes. Transfer the meat to a roasting pan and roast in the oven until a meat thermometer inserted in the center of the fillet registers 120°F (50°C), about 10–15 minutes. Let the meat rest on a carving board, covered with aluminum foil, for 15 minutes, then slice thin. Serve with the hot-sweet mustard.

RICE & WILD RICE SALAD

SERVES 6 (MULTIPLY BY 3 FOR BUFFET)

Subtly perfumed basmati rice and nutlike wild rice combine with a sweetly spiced dressing for this flavorful salad.

FOR THE RICE:

4 cups (32 fl oz/1 l) cold water
4 teaspoons salt
½ cup (3 oz/90 g) wild rice
1½ cups (10 oz/315 g) basmati rice
one 2-inch (5-cm) piece fresh ginger

FOR THE VINAIGRETTE:

½ teaspoon ground nutmeg
½ teaspoon ground cumin
2–3 tablespoons fresh lemon juice
½ cup (4 fl oz/125 ml) olive oil or peanut oil
salt and freshly ground pepper to taste

TO FINISH THE SALAD:

½ cup (1½ oz/45 g) chopped green (spring) onions
½ cup (3 oz/90 g) dried currants, soaked in ½ cup (4 fl oz/125 ml) Marsala until soft (10–20 minutes)
⅓ cup (2 oz/60 g) toasted pine nuts or slivered almonds (see glossary)

To cook the rice, bring 1½ cups (12 fl oz/375 ml) of the water and 2 teaspoons of the salt to a boil in a medium saucepan. Add the wild rice, reduce heat to low, cover and simmer until the rice is tender, about 1 hour.

Combine the basmati rice and the remaining 2½ cups (20 fl oz/625 ml) water in a medium saucepan. Let sit for 1 hour. Then bring to a boil, add the remaining 2 teaspoons salt and the ginger, reduce heat to low, cover and simmer until the rice has absorbed all of the water and is tender, about 15 minutes. Discard the ginger.

To make the vinaigrette, combine the nutmeg and cumin in a small bowl and whisk in the lemon juice. Add the oil and season with salt and pepper.

To finish the salad, combine the wild rice and basmati rice while still warm in a large bowl. Toss the vinaigrette with the rice, then stir in the green onions, currants and any remaining Marsala, and nuts. Adjust the seasoning. Serve at room temperature.

Serve any extra rice salad in a bowl alongside the beef.

TUNA WITH PEPPERS & OLIVES

SERVES 6 (MULTIPLY BY 2 FOR BUFFET)

Make this easy Mediterranean-style salad up to 3 hours ahead to let the flavors mingle.

1 lb (500 g) fresh tuna, cut about 1 inch (2.5 cm) thick, or canned solid-pack tuna in oil or water, drained
2 red bell peppers (capsicums)
2 yellow bell peppers (capsicums)
¾ cup (6 fl oz/180 ml) olive oil
¼ cup (2 fl oz/60 ml) red wine vinegar or more to taste
1 tablespoon minced garlic
2 tablespoons minced anchovy
⅓ cup (2 oz/60 g) capers, rinsed and coarsely chopped
freshly ground pepper to taste
arugula for lining plate, optional
½ cup (2½ oz/75 g) pitted black olives, such as Kalamata, halved
⅓ cup (½ oz/15 g) chopped fresh flat-leaf (Italian) parsley

If using fresh tuna, place the fillet in an oiled baking dish, cover tightly with aluminum foil and bake in a preheated 450°F (230°C) oven until it is barely pink and still moist in the center, about 8–10 minutes. Remove and let cool. Meanwhile, roast, peel and derib the peppers as directed on page 189. Slice the peppers into thin strips.

Break the cooked or canned tuna into chunks and place in a bowl. In a separate bowl, combine the oil, vinegar, garlic, anchovy and capers. Season with pepper and pour half of this over the tuna. Toss well. Toss the peppers with the remaining vinaigrette. Spread the peppers on a platter lined with arugula, if using, and top the peppers with the tuna; garnish with the olives and parsley.

BERRY TIRAMISÙ

SERVES 12 (MAKE 2 CAKES FOR BUFFET)

This popular Italian dessert gains fresh new flavor from ripe berries. For easier slicing, make and weight the tiramisù the night before. Serve the berry sauce alongside.

FOR THE GÉNOISE:

6 eggs

1 cup (8 oz/250 g) granulated sugar

1 teaspoon vanilla extract (essence)

1 teaspoon grated lemon zest

1 cup (4 oz/125 g) cake (soft-wheat)
 flour, sifted

6 tablespoons (3 oz/90 g) unsalted
 butter, melted

FOR THE CUSTARD FILLING:

5 eggs, separated

⅓ cup (3 oz/90 g) granulated sugar

1 lb (500 g) Mascarpone cheese at
 room temperature

2 tablespoons dark rum or Marsala

1 teaspoon vanilla extract (essence)

FOR THE BERRY FILLING:

4 cups (1 lb/500 g) raspberries or
 sliced strawberries

¼ cup (2 fl oz/60 ml) dark rum
 or Marsala

2 tablespoons granulated sugar

FOR THE BERRY SAUCE:

1 cup (4 oz/125 g) raspberries or
 strawberries

¼ cup (2 oz/60 g) granulated sugar

1 teaspoon vanilla extract (essence)

FOR THE GARNISH:

confectioners' (icing) sugar

12 whole raspberries or strawberries

To make the génoise, preheat an oven to 350°F (180°C). Butter a 9-inch (23-cm) cake pan and line the bottom with baking parchment.

❧ Place the eggs and sugar in the bowl of an electric mixer, set the bowl over hot water and whisk for a few minutes until warm to the touch. Remove from the hot water and beat on high speed with the whisk attachment until very thick and pale and a small amount trailed from the whisk forms a ribbon on the surface of the mixture, about 8 minutes. Stir in the vanilla and lemon zest. With a spatula, gently fold in half the sifted flour, then the melted butter, then the remaining flour. Pour into the prepared pan, tap the pan lightly on the counter to level the batter and bake on the middle rack of the oven until a toothpick inserted in the center of the cake comes out clean, about 30 minutes. Turn the cake out onto a rack to cool. When cool, cut the génoise into 3 layers with a serrated knife.

❧ To make the custard filling, in the bowl of an electric mixer whisk the egg yolks and half the sugar over hot water for a few minutes until warm to the touch. Remove from the hot water and beat on high speed with the whisk attachment until thick, pale and fluffy, about 8–10 minutes.

❧ Mix the Mascarpone with a fork to make sure it is smooth. Fold the Mascarpone into the yolks and sugar, then fold in the rum or Marsala and the vanilla. In a large bowl, beat the egg whites for a few minutes until foamy. Gradually beat in the remaining sugar until soft peaks form, about 1 minute longer. Do not overbeat. Fold the whites into the Mascarpone mixture.

❧ To make the berry filling, mix the berries with the dark rum or Marsala and the sugar and let stand for 10 minutes.

❧ To assemble, place 1 layer of the génoise in the bottom of a 9-inch (23-cm) springform pan. Top evenly with

half of the berry filling. Spoon half of the custard over the berries. Place another third of the génoise over the custard and add the remaining filling, then the remaining custard, then the remaining génoise. Wrap the pan with aluminum foil. Weight the cake with several plates and refrigerate overnight.

❧ To prepare the berry sauce, purée the berries, sugar and vanilla in a food processor or blender. Strain out the berry seeds and chill the sauce until serving time.

❧ Immediately before serving, remove the sides from the springform pan and place the cake on a serving plate. Sprinkle the top with confectioners' sugar, garnish with the whole berries and serve with the berry sauce.

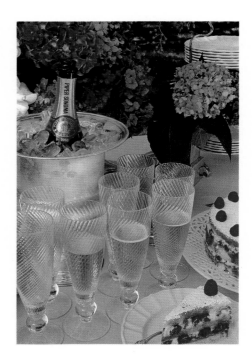

For serving the sparkling wine that accompanies the dessert, your most elegant Champagne flutes and a silver cooler add festivity to the celebration.

Berry Tiramisù

TEATIME FÊTE

A TEATIME GATHERING in a garden, on a porch or in a sun-room can be both lighthearted and serene. Lighthearted because it may celebrate an engagement, a bridal or baby shower, the birthday of a special friend or a family member. Serene because tea is steeped in tradition, evoking an era past.

To complement the freshness of this menu, we used crisp linen tablecloths and napkins, floral-patterned dishware and an abundance of colorful roses and tulips. To encourage guests to mingle and to promote easy conversation, we arranged a variety of seating areas and separate serving tables for the assorted foods and beverages. The cakes, cookies and peaches could be arranged in one area while the sandwiches and their accompaniments could be set on another table, or even in a nearby room. Be sure to provide enough comfortable chairs and cushions for every guest to have a seat.

THE TEATIME MENU for twelve that follows is purposefully light, combining contemporary tastes and old-fashioned dishes. You could offer guests a choice of teas, such as Orange Pekoe or smoky Lapsang souchong to go with the sandwiches, and a scented Earl Grey or herbal teas with the sweets. Lemonade and wine spritzers are good alternatives for guests who prefer other drinks.

These recipes are readily adaptable for other meals, too. The sandwiches, cookies and madeleines are excellent at lunchtime or in a picnic basket. Try the conserve and tea bread at breakfast or brunch and the peaches for dessert at any time.

Menu

Strewn rose petals add a lovely, festive touch to the tea table. Arrange teaspoons in a small vase or sugar bowl.

WINE RECOMMENDATIONS

While freshly brewed tea will be poured, wine may also be offered in some form. Spritzers composed of equal parts wine and sparkling water, served over ice with a citrus slice, make a very refreshing drink; try using a slightly sweet wine such as Chenin Blanc or white Zinfandel. With the sandwiches, offer a simple white wine of light to medium body, such as French Mâcon-Villages or a Sancerre.

*Lemon Saffron Tea Bread
with Spiced Blueberry Conserve*

*Tuna Pâté
with Sun-dried Tomatoes*

Pitas with Feta, Walnuts & Aïoli

*Tomato, Tapenade &
Mozzarella Sandwiches*

Jennifer's Chocolate Dream Cookies

Ginger-Orange Madeleines

Peaches in Wine

Long-stemmed Strawberries

*If presents are brought for a guest of honor, display
them prominently on a nearby chair or table.*

PREPARATION LIST

◆ Several months to 1 day ahead, make the
blueberry conserve.

◆ Up to a week ahead, make the tapenade.

◆ The day before, make the tea bread, the
madeleines and the cookies.

◆ The night before, prepare the tuna pâté.

◆ Up to 4 hours ahead, prepare the
pita sandwiches.

◆ One hour ahead, prepare the peaches.

THIS MENU SERVES 12. FOR A SMALLER
GROUP, SERVE FEWER DISHES.

*Lace-cap hydrangeas,
their pots decorated
with pretty ribbon
bows, make charming
host or hostess gifts.*

LEMON SAFFRON TEA BREAD

MAKES ONE 9- BY 5- BY 3-INCH
(23- BY 13- BY 7.5-CM) LOAF

Crushed saffron gives this bread an intense yellow color and subtle perfume. See the glossary for directions on how to crush it.

2 cups (10 oz/315 g) all-purpose
 (plain) flour
2 teaspoons baking powder
1 teaspoon salt
¼ teaspoon baking soda (bicarbonate
 of soda)
½ cup (4 oz/125 g) unsalted butter at
 room temperature
¾ cup (6 oz/185 g) sugar
2 eggs
1 tablespoon grated lemon zest
¼ teaspoon saffron threads crushed
 and steeped in 2 tablespoons fresh
 lemon juice
¾ cup (6 fl oz/180 ml) milk
½ cup (2 oz/60 g) coarsely
 chopped walnuts

Preheat an oven to 350°F (180°C). Butter and flour a 9- by 5- by 3-inch (23- by 13- by 7.5-cm) loaf pan.
ò Sift together the flour, baking powder, salt and baking soda and set aside. In a large bowl, beat the butter and sugar together until fluffy. Beat in the eggs, lemon zest and saffron mixture. With a rubber spatula, fold a third of the dry ingredients, then half the milk into the butter mixture; repeat, ending with the dry ingredients. Mix in the walnuts and pour into the prepared loaf pan.
ò Bake on the middle rack of the oven until a skewer inserted in the center of the loaf comes out clean, about 1 hour. Let cool in the pan on a rack for 10 minutes, then turn out onto the rack to cool completely. Wrap the bread in plastic and let sit overnight to mellow. Slice thinly to serve.

A doll-size tea set is displayed as a fitting decoration on a side table.

SPICED BLUEBERRY CONSERVE

MAKES ABOUT 5 CUPS (40 OZ/1.2 KG)

Sweet spices, citrus zest and a splash of cider vinegar contribute extra flavor and tang to this thick-textured preserve.

4 cups (1 lb/500 g) fresh or thawed
 frozen whole blueberries
3 cups (1½ lb/750 g) sugar
½ teaspoon ground cinnamon
¼ teaspoon ground allspice
¼ cup (2 fl oz/60 ml) cider vinegar
¼ cup (2 fl oz/60 ml) fresh lemon juice
grated zest of 1 lemon
grated zest of 1 orange, optional

In a large, heavy enameled or stainless-steel pot, combine all of the ingredients and bring to a boil. Reduce the heat and simmer, uncovered and stirring occasionally, until thickened, about 25 minutes. This jam sets up fast; it is done when a teaspoonful is still a little runny when dropped on a chilled plate.
ò Pour into 5 hot sterilized 1-cup (8-fl oz/250-ml) canning jars, leaving about ½ inch (12 mm) of head space, then seal the jars. Process in a hot-water bath for 10 minutes (see Canning, page 186), or store in the refrigerator for up to 3 months.

*Lemon Saffron Tea Bread;
Spiced Blueberry Conserve*

TUNA PÂTÉ WITH SUN-DRIED TOMATOES

MAKES ABOUT 24 OPEN-FACED SANDWICHES

Sun-dried tomatoes, red onion and fresh basil brighten the taste and color of this simple spread. If you wish to make your own country bread, see the recipe on page 176.

FOR THE TUNA PÂTÉ:

1 lb (500 g) fresh tuna, cut about 1 inch (2.5 cm) thick, or canned solid-pack tuna in oil or water, drained
¼ cup (2 fl oz/60 ml) fresh lemon juice
⅔ cup (3 oz/90 g) finely chopped red (Spanish) onion
about 1 cup (8 fl oz/250 ml) mayonnaise
½ cup (4 oz/125 g) finely chopped sun-dried tomatoes
¼ cup (⅜ oz/10 g) chopped fresh basil
salt and freshly ground pepper to taste

FOR THE SANDWICHES:

1 cup (1½ oz/40 g) lightly packed fresh basil leaves
¼ cup (1 oz/30 g) freshly grated Parmesan cheese
3 tablespoons pine nuts
2 cloves garlic
½ cup (4 fl oz/125 ml) olive oil
12 large slices focaccia or country bread
paper-thin lemon slices

To make the pâté: If using fresh tuna, place the fillet in an oiled baking dish, cover tightly with aluminum foil and bake in a preheated 450°F (230°C) oven until it is barely pink and still moist in the center, about 8–10 minutes. Remove and let cool. Mash the cooked

Tuna Pâté with Sun-dried Tomatoes; Tomato, Tapenade & Mozzarella Sandwiches; Pitas with Feta, Walnuts & Aïoli

or canned tuna with a fork or pulse briefly in a food processor. Transfer to a bowl and add the lemon juice, red onion, mayonnaise, sun-dried tomatoes and chopped basil and mix until you have a spreadable consistency. Season with salt and pepper. Cover and refrigerate until ready to use, up to 8 hours.

❧ To make the sandwiches, process the basil leaves, cheese, pine nuts, garlic and oil in a blender or food processor until smooth. Cut the focaccia or country bread slices into small squares, then top with the basil mixture and the tuna pâté. Serve open-faced. Garnish with lemon.

PITAS WITH FETA, WALNUTS & AÏOLI

MAKES 12 PITA SANDWICH HALVES, OR 24 MINI PITAS

A vivid combination of tastes, textures and colors goes into these sandwiches. If made ahead, cover them with a clean, damp cloth to keep the pita moist.

6 pita bread rounds, or 24 mini pitas
about ½ cup (4 fl oz/125 ml) aïoli (recipe on page 174)
24 large watercress sprigs
36 large fresh mint leaves
1 lb (500 g) feta cheese, cut into 12 thin slices
1½ cups (6 oz/185 g) chopped walnuts
6 red bell peppers (capsicums), roasted, peeled and chopped (see glossary)

Cut the pita rounds in half and carefully open the pockets (for mini pitas, slice off the top third of the pita rounds and open the pocket). Spread the aïoli inside the pitas. Into each sandwich, tuck even amounts of watercress, mint, feta, walnuts and bell peppers. If desired, cover and refrigerate the sandwiches until ready to serve, up to 4 hours.

TOMATO, TAPENADE & MOZZARELLA SANDWICHES

MAKES 24 SMALL SANDWICHES

Tapenade, a pungent niçoise olive spread, can be made ahead and refrigerated for up to 1 week. A recipe for homemade baguettes appears on page 176.

FOR THE TAPENADE:

1 cup (5 oz/155 g) pitted green or black niçoise olives
2 tablespoons chopped rinsed capers
1 tablespoon minced garlic
2 teaspoons chopped anchovies
½ teaspoon freshly ground pepper
1 teaspoon grated orange or lemon zest
pinch of red pepper flakes, optional
4–6 tablespoons (2–3 fl oz/60–90 ml) olive oil

FOR THE SANDWICHES:

1 long baguette (about 1 lb/500 g)
6–8 plum (Roma) tomatoes, sliced
two 8-ounce (250-g) balls fresh mozzarella cheese, sliced
24 arugula leaves

To make the tapenade, combine the olives, capers, garlic, anchovies, ground pepper, zest and optional red pepper flakes in a food processor or blender. Purée, pouring in enough oil to make a thick spread. Makes 1 cup (8 fl oz/250 ml).

❧ To make the sandwiches, cut the baguette in half lengthwise, then cut each half into 12 diagonal slices. Spread each slice with tapenade. Top each piece equally with sliced tomatoes, sliced mozzarella cheese and an arugula leaf. Serve open-faced.

JENNIFER'S CHOCOLATE DREAM COOKIES

MAKES 48 COOKIES

Light and crackly on the outside, soft and chewy within, these cookies are reminiscent of good chocolate fudge.

2 cups (10 oz/315 g) all-purpose
  (plain) flour
¾ cup (3 oz/90 g) sifted cocoa
2 teaspoons baking powder
1 teaspoon salt
1 cup (8 oz/250 g) unsalted butter at
  room temperature
1 cup (7 oz/220 g) dark brown
  sugar, packed
1 cup (8 oz/250 g) granulated sugar
2 teaspoons vanilla extract (essence)
2 eggs
6 oz (185 g) bittersweet chocolate,
  coarsely chopped, or bittersweet
  chocolate chips

Preheat an oven to 325°F (170°C). Line 2 baking sheets with baking parchment. Sift the flour, cocoa, baking powder and salt together into a medium bowl.
ᔑ In a large bowl, beat the butter, brown sugar and granulated sugar together until fluffy. Add the vanilla and eggs and beat well. Stir in the flour-cocoa mixture, then fold in the chocolate chunks.
ᔑ Drop the cookie dough by the tablespoonful onto the prepared baking sheets. Bake until the cookies are puffed and set but still chewy in the middle, about 8–10 minutes. Let cool on racks. If made ahead, store in a plastic container until ready to use.

GINGER-ORANGE MADELEINES

MAKES 36 MADELEINES

These delicate little sponge cakes gain subtle flavor from orange zest and candied ginger. If you don't have enough madeleine pans, bake them in batches.

3 eggs
2 egg yolks
pinch of salt
¾ cup (6 oz/185 g) granulated sugar
2 tablespoons grated orange zest soaked
  in 3 tablespoons orange juice
1¼ cups (5 oz/155 g) sifted all-purpose
  (plain) flour
¼ cup (1 oz/30 g) finely chopped
  candied ginger
½ cup (4 oz/125 g) plus 2 tablespoons
  unsalted butter, clarified (see glossary)
confectioners' (icing) sugar for sprinkling

Preheat an oven to 350°F (180°C). Butter and lightly flour 4 standard madeleine pans (or fewer, if necessary).
ᔑ Place the whole eggs, egg yolks and granulated sugar together in the bowl of an electric mixer, set the bowl over hot water and whisk for a few minutes until warm to the touch. Remove from the hot water, add the salt and beat on high speed until the mixture is very thick and pale. Add the orange zest and juice and beat well. Sift the flour over the batter and fold it in, then fold in the ginger. Finally, fold in the butter a little at a time. Fill the molds two-thirds of the way full with batter, then bake until golden, about 15 minutes.
ᔑ Gently loosen the sides of the madeleines from the molds and turn them out onto a rack. Sprinkle the ribbed sides with confectioners' sugar while still warm.

If you want to offer a selection of teas, provide a few individual pots and tea strainers so that a guest can pour his or her own cupful.

Ginger-Orange Madeleines;
Jennifer's Chocolate Dream Cookies

PEACHES IN WINE

SERVES 12

For such elegant results, the preparation of this light dessert could not be simpler. Nectarines also work well.

12 ripe peaches
4 cups (32 fl oz/1 l) fruity white wine such as Asti Spumante, Moscato or Riesling, or a light, fruity red wine such as Lambrusco or Beaujolais
1 cup (8 oz/250 g) sugar

*B*ring a large pot of water to a boil. Drop in a few peaches at a time for 5 seconds to loosen the skin. Lift out with a slotted spoon, let cool briefly, then peel. Cut the peaches in half and remove the pits.

&> Combine the wine and sugar in an attractive glass bowl; stir until the sugar dissolves. Slice the peaches and place them in the wine. Chill for 1 hour, then serve.

*R*efreshing lemonade, offered
in tall glasses over ice,
is a delicious beverage to offer
in addition to tea.

Peaches in Wine

AL FRESCO LUNCH

WARM WEATHER BRINGS the irresistible urge to eat out-doors. While that usually means a casual barbecue or picnic, you might want to try a sit-down, open-air lunch. You'll find plenty of reasons to serve this menu: summer holidays, birthdays, end-of-the-weekend send-offs.

A beachside getaway is an ideal location, with the table set up in or near the sand, but this menu is equally appropriate served on a deck or even in a sunny room at home. To contrast with the casual outdoor setting, we dressed the table with good china, silver, crystal and linens, and folded the napkins into bishop's hats (page 183). Director's chairs pro-vided informal seating. Taking advantage of the seaside locale, we scattered shells and sand dollars on the table and placed sea grass in vases filled with sand and smooth stones; if you're not at the beach, other greenery will do.

Package shortcake biscuits in decorated bags as gifts for guests.

Menu

INSPIRED BY NEW ENGLAND cuisine, our al fresco lunch features summertime favorites such as lobster, sweet corn, maple syrup and fresh blueberries. All the recipes are easily prepared, since much of the work may be done in advance and the last-minute cooking is limited primarily to the main course. With a few substitutions, these recipes can be made anywhere and at any time of year.

To mark this unique occasion, you might want to bake an extra batch of dessert short-cakes and package them in paper bags tied with raffia or twine for guests to take home. Try knotting shells onto the ties as a reminder of the seaside theme.

A tray holds small glasses of chilled ruby port to accompany the shortcakes for dessert.

MAPLE SYRUP— & MUSTARD-GLAZED POUSSINS

SERVES 6

Take care not to overcook these little chickens: When done, their flesh remains slightly pink. Another time, try quail.

6 poussins or Cornish hens, about 1 lb (500 g) each, or 12 quail
2 teaspoons dry mustard
½ teaspoon ground cinnamon
2 tablespoons cider vinegar
⅔ cup (5 fl oz/160 ml) maple syrup
3 tablespoons prepared Dijon mustard
2 tablespoons soy sauce
salt and freshly ground pepper to taste
oil for brushing

*B*utterfly the poussins or Cornish hens: Insert a sharp knife through the neck cavity of each bird and carefully cut down one side of the backbone. Cut along the other side of the backbone to remove it from the body. Press on the breastbone of each bird to flatten it. (You may leave the quail whole.)

&❧ In a bowl, combine the dry mustard, cinnamon and vinegar and mix into a paste. Add the maple syrup, prepared mustard and soy sauce and adjust the seasoning; it should be spicy but sweet. Spread half of this mixture evenly over the birds, cover and let sit at room temperature for 1 hour or refrigerate for up to 8 hours. Reserve the remaining half of the paste for basting.

&❧ Preheat a broiler (griller). Or, prepare a fire in a grill; position the oiled grill rack 4–6 inches (10–15 cm) above the fire. Sprinkle the birds with salt and pepper and brush with a little oil. Broil the poussins or hens, or grill them over medium-hot coals, flesh-side down for 5 minutes, then brush with the glaze, turn and cook for 5 minutes longer. (Cook quail for 3–4 minutes on each side.)

FRESH CORN & POLENTA CAKES

SERVES 6

Look for polenta in a well-stocked food shop or an Italian grocer. When cooked and cooled, it can be cut into any shape.

4 ears corn or 3 cups (1¼ lb/625 g) thawed frozen corn kernels
1½ cups (9 oz/280 g) polenta or coarse yellow cornmeal
6 cups (48 fl oz/1.5 l) cold water or more as needed
salt and freshly ground pepper to taste
about ½ cup (4 fl oz/125 ml) olive oil or vegetable oil
minced fresh chives

*I*f using ears of corn, cut the kernels off the ears with a large knife. Drop the corn kernels into boiling salted water and cook for 1–2 minutes. Drain the corn and rinse in cold water. Dry very well on paper towels.

&❧ Combine the polenta or cornmeal and cold water in a large saucepan. Cook over low heat, stirring often, until thick and no longer grainy on the tongue, 20–30 minutes. Add more water gradually if the polenta is thick but still grainy. When the polenta is done, stir in the corn kernels. Season with salt and pepper and spread in an even layer in an oiled baking sheet with sides; the polenta should be about ¾ inch (2 cm) thick. Cover with plastic wrap and refrigerate until firm.

&❧ To serve, cut the polenta into circles, triangles or rectangles. Heat the oil in a frying pan to a depth of ¼ inch (6 mm) and sauté the polenta pieces until pale gold on both sides, about 5 minutes total. Transfer to plates and sprinkle with chives.

HONEY-BAKED TOMATOES WITH CRUSTY TOPPING

SERVES 6

Basting with honey highlights the natural sweetness of these baked tomatoes. If desired, place each tomato on a plate with a handful of fresh watercress or arugula sprigs for a refreshingly bitter contrast.

1½ cups (3 oz/90 g) fresh bread crumbs
½ cup (4 fl oz/125 ml) olive oil
1 teaspoon salt
½ teaspoon freshly ground pepper
6 tablespoons (4 oz/125 g) honey
pinch of ground nutmeg
6 ripe tomatoes

*P*reheat an oven to 350°F (180°C). Spread the bread crumbs on a baking sheet, toss with 6 tablespoons (3 fl oz/ 90 ml) of the oil and sprinkle with ½ teaspoon of the salt and the pepper. Bake, stirring often, until golden and slightly crunchy but not hard, about 20 minutes. Set aside, leaving the oven on.

&❧ In a small saucepan over low heat, warm the honey, remaining 2 tablespoons of oil and the nutmeg.

&❧ Cut a slice off the stem end of each tomato. Place the tomatoes in a baking dish. Sprinkle with the remaining ½ teaspoon salt, brush the top of each tomato with a little of the honey mixture and top each tomato with some of the bread crumbs, pressing them into the tomato. Bake the tomatoes until soft and lightly browned on top, basting with the honey mixture several times, about 15–20 minutes.

*Maple Syrup— & Mustard-glazed Poussins;
Fresh Corn & Polenta Cakes;
Honey-baked Tomatoes with Crusty Topping*

SPICED PEACHES

MAKES 12 PEACHES

A classic American conserve, these keep for up to a month in the refrigerator or up to a year when canned. Serve them with the main course, cut in half, pitted and garnished with watercress.

1½ cups (12 fl oz/375 ml) cider
   vinegar
1½ cups (12 fl oz/375 ml) water
2 cups (1 lb/500 g) sugar
3 sticks cinnamon
10–12 whole cloves
1 teaspoon black peppercorns
2 strips lemon zest
12 firm ripe peaches

Combine the vinegar, water, sugar, cinnamon, cloves, peppercorns and lemon zest in a large, deep enameled or stainless-steel saucepan. Bring to a boil and stir until the sugar dissolves. Reduce the heat and simmer the syrup for 10 minutes.

❧ Meanwhile, drop a few peaches at a time into a large pot of boiling water for 1–2 minutes to loosen the skin. Lift out with a slotted spoon, let cool briefly, then peel. Add the peaches to the hot syrup and poach for 2 minutes, then remove them with a slotted spoon and place in 2 sterilized 4-cup (32–fl oz/1-l) canning jars. Spoon the syrup over the peaches to within ½ inch (12 mm) of the top and seal the jars. Process in a hot-water bath for 25–30 minutes (see Canning, page 186), or store in the refrigerator for up to 1 month.

Spiced Peaches

Cluster sea treasures in a half shell.

WARM BLUEBERRY SHORTCAKES

SERVES 6

Classic cream biscuits accompany this variation on strawberry shortcake.

FOR THE SHORTCAKES:

1¾ cups (9 oz/280 g) all-purpose (plain) flour

½ teaspoon salt

1 tablespoon baking powder

2 teaspoons sugar

6 tablespoons (3 oz/90 g) unsalted butter or vegetable shortening (vegetable lard), chilled

1 cup (8 fl oz/250 ml) milk or heavy (double) cream

grated zest of 1 orange or 2 lemons

about 3 tablespoons unsalted butter, melted, or heavy (double) cream

FOR THE BLUEBERRY COMPOTE:

6 cups (1½ lb/750 g) fresh or thawed frozen whole blueberries

2 tablespoons fresh lemon juice

1 teaspoon ground cinnamon

1½ cups (12 oz/375 g) sugar

grated zest of 1 lemon or 1 orange

FOR THE MAPLE WHIPPED CREAM:

1 cup (8 fl oz/250 ml) heavy (double) cream

2 tablespoons maple syrup

¼ teaspoon vanilla extract (essence)

Preheat an oven to 450°F (230°C). To make the shortcakes, combine the flour, salt, baking powder and sugar in a medium bowl. Cut the butter or shortening into bits, then blend into the flour mixture with a pastry cutter or 2 knives until the mixture resembles cornmeal. Make a well in the center and add the milk or cream and zest. Stir quickly until the dough comes free from the sides of the bowl, about 1 minute. Turn the dough out onto a lightly floured board and knead gently and quickly, turning it about 12 times, or until the dough is no longer sticky. Pat into a ½-inch-thick (12-mm) square.

❧ Dipping a 2¼-inch (5.5-cm) cutter into flour each time, cut the dough into 12 round or square biscuits. Place on an ungreased baking sheet, brush the tops with the melted butter or the cream and bake on the middle rack of the oven until pale gold, 12–15 minutes.

❧ Meanwhile, to make the compote, combine 4 cups (1 lb/500 g) of the blueberries with the lemon juice, cinnamon, sugar and zest in a heavy saucepan over moderate heat. Simmer until thickened and hot, about 5 minutes. Stir in the remaining blueberries and set aside.

❧ To make the maple whipped cream, in a bowl beat the cream, maple syrup and vanilla until it forms soft peaks.

❧ To serve, split the warm biscuits in half crosswise. Place 2 bottoms on each of 6 individual plates. Spoon half of the blueberry compote on the biscuits, add a dollop of whipped cream and a little more compote to each, then top with the remaining biscuit halves. Spoon on remaining compote and serve at once.

Warm Blueberry Shortcakes

POOLSIDE FIESTA

TRADITIONAL SUMMER HOLIDAYS and other special events at the height of the season call for high-spirited entertaining. To beat the heat, plan the party for late in the day, when evening breezes begin to stir. A deck beside a swimming pool is a perfect spot, but any patio, large balcony, airy dining room, or picnic area in the country will do.

The Latin tastes of this menu inspired us to assemble the hottest-colored accessories we could find: heavy, peasant-style pottery and coarse linens in reds, yellows, greens and blues. We chose flowers from the same palette, added bouquets of fresh chili peppers and arranged them in brightly colored Latin American food tins (found in ethnic markets). The tables were draped with woven Mexican rugs and chairs of all kinds were pressed into use for seating around large outdoor dining tables set end to end.

Empty colorful food tins are used to display pepper bouquets.

Menu

A POOLSIDE FIESTA is the natural setting for a menu of easily prepared, quickly grilled foods with enough variety to please everyone. The recipes that follow take their inspiration from *churrascos*, the traditional outdoor barbecues of Argentina and Brazil. These spicy, but not-too-hot dishes, complemented by icy rum cocktails, beer or wine, are perfect for any summer party.

To make inexpensive table decorations, try scoring the peels of lemons, limes and oranges in decorative patterns with a citrus zester; tie napkins with bright ribbons knotted around the stems of fresh chilies. Place tropical fruits, such as papayas and pineapples, down the center of the table and use whole bell peppers, their stems cut out, as colorful holders for votive candles to light the table as evening falls on this memorable celebration.

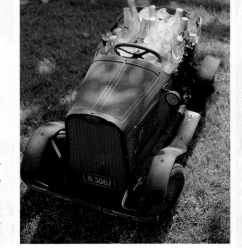

Lined with heavy-duty plastic bags and filled with ice, an old toy pedal car or a wagon makes a whimsical vehicle for chilling beer, wine or other beverages.

Caipirinha Cocktail & Pineapple Batida

*Latin American Fish Brochettes
with Peanut-Tomato Salsa*

❧

Grilled Steaks with Chimichurri Sauce

Tomatoes with Avocado Salsa

Latin American Potato Salad

Grilled Peppered Bananas with Bacon

*Grilled Corn on the Cob
with Chili-Lime Butter*

❧

Caipirinha (Rum & Lime Cream) Pie

WINE RECOMMENDATIONS

Though some guests may continue to sip their cock-tails with the first course, offer a light red wine such as a young Beaujolais or a Pinot Noir. With the steaks, pour a bold, country-style red: American Zinfandel or Chilean Cabernet Sauvignon. Beer, of course, is also good throughout the meal and Asti Spumante or Muscat would be refreshing with dessert.

PREPARATION LIST

◆ Up to 8 hours ahead, make the pie, cover and refrigerate; marinate the steaks.

◆ Up to 5 hours ahead, make the peanut-tomato salsa for the fish and the chimichurri sauce for the meat.

◆ Up to 3 hours before, butter, wrap and refrigerate the corn; mix and refrigerate the potato salad.

◆ Two hours ahead, make the avocado salsa.

◆ One hour before, preheat the grill; wrap the bananas in bacon; marinate the fish.

EACH FOOD RECIPE YIELDS 12 SERVINGS. MAKE THE DRINKS IN BATCHES OF 2, AS NOT EVERY-ONE WILL BE CONSUMING HARD LIQUOR.

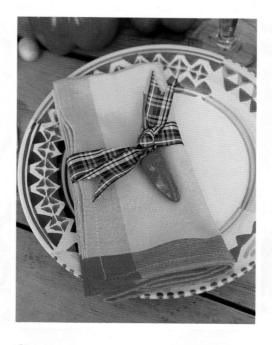

Spice up your table with a chili pepper and a ribbon knotted around each napkin.

CAIPIRINHA COCKTAIL

MAKES 2 DRINKS

A national drink of Brazil, this lime-and-rum cocktail packs a wallop and is great with spicy foods. Serve with chunks of lime in each glass.

1 juicy lime, cut into 6 pieces
2 heaping teaspoons confectioners'
   (icing) or superfine (caster) sugar
2 shot glasses (3 fl oz/90 ml) cachaça
   (Brazilian sugarcane rum) or light rum
2 cups (10 oz/315 g) ice cubes

*P*lace the lime in a beverage shaker and press down hard on it with a pestle or a wooden spoon to mash the pulp and release the juice. Add the rest of the ingredients and shake well. Pour the liquid, lime, ice and all into tall glasses.

PINEAPPLE BATIDA

MAKES 2 DRINKS

Batida *means "beaten" in Portuguese—an apt description for this frothy tropical punch.*

⅓ cup (3 fl oz/90 ml) pineapple juice
4 teaspoons superfine (caster) sugar
2 tablespoons fresh lemon juice
2 shot glasses (3 fl oz/90 ml) cachaça
   (Brazilian sugarcane rum) or light rum
2 cups (10 oz/315 g) ice cubes

*C*ombine all of the ingredients in a shaker and shake well. Pour the liquid and ice cubes into tall glasses.

LATIN AMERICAN FISH BROCHETTES WITH PEANUT-TOMATO SALSA

SERVES 12

Don't marinate these appetizers more than an hour, or the citrus juices will "cook" the fish like a ceviche. Use swordfish, halibut, mahi-mahi or seabass.

FOR THE SALSA:

½ cup (2½ oz/75 g) roasted peanuts
   (salted or unsalted), coarsely chopped
2 cups (12 oz/375 g) finely chopped
   peeled, seeded tomatoes
½ cup (2½ oz/75 g) minced onions
½ cup (4 fl oz/125 ml) fresh lemon juice
2 cloves garlic, minced
3 jalapeño (hot green) chili peppers,
   seeded and minced
1–2 tablespoons finely grated fresh
   ginger or to taste
2 tablespoons chopped cilantro
   (fresh coriander)
½ cup (4 fl oz/125 ml) olive oil

FOR THE BROCHETTES:

3 lb (1.5 kg) firm white-fleshed fish or
   48 large shrimp (prawns)
8 cloves garlic, minced
3–4 jalapeño (hot green) chili peppers,
   seeded and minced, or ½ teaspoon
   or more cayenne pepper
2 tablespoons ground cumin
2 tablespoons ground coriander
½ cup (4 fl oz/125 ml) fresh lemon or
   lime juice or red wine vinegar
½ cup (4 fl oz/125 ml) olive oil
salt and freshly ground pepper to taste

*T*o make the salsa, combine all of the ingredients in a medium bowl; cover and set aside for up to 5 hours.
❧ To prepare the brochettes, cut the fish into 1-inch (2.5-cm) cubes or, if you are using shrimp, shell and devein them. In a small bowl, mix the garlic,

jalapeños, cumin and coriander into a paste with the lemon juice (or lime juice or vinegar). Whisk in the oil. Place the fish or shrimp in a glass or plastic container, pour the marinade over and toss. Cover and marinate in the refrigerator for 30–60 minutes, stirring once or twice.
❧ Meanwhile, prepare a fire in a grill. Position the oiled grill rack 4–6 inches (10–15 cm) above the fire. Or, preheat a broiler (griller).
❧ Remove the fish or shrimp from the marinade and thread on 12 skewers. Sprinkle with salt and pepper. Grill over hot coals or broil until the fish turns opaque in the center or until the shrimp are pink, about 2 minutes on each side. Serve with the salsa.

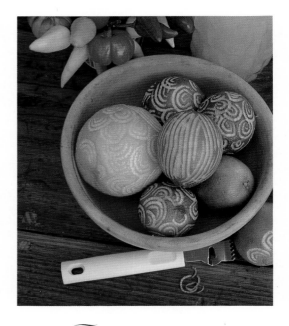

*F*or a natural decoration, use a zesting tool to score folk-art-style designs on citrus fruits.

*C*aipirinha Cocktail; Pineapple Batida; Latin American Fish Brochettes with Peanut-Tomato Salsa

GRILLED STEAKS WITH CHIMICHURRI SAUCE

SERVES 12

Chimichurri, a traditional Argentine table sauce for grilled meat, is also excellent on grilled chicken or seafood.

FOR THE CHIMICHURRI SAUCE:
1 cup (8 fl oz/250 ml) olive oil
½ cup (4 fl oz/125 ml) red
 wine vinegar
½ cup (4 fl oz/125 ml) fresh
 orange juice
grated zest of 1 orange
1 cup (5 oz/155 g) minced onions
1 tablespoon minced garlic
½ cup (¾ oz/20 g) minced
 fresh parsley
1 tablespoon dried oregano
1 teaspoon cayenne pepper

FOR THE STEAKS:
3 large onions, finely chopped
8 cloves garlic, minced
3 tablespoons chili powder
2 tablespoons ground cumin
2 tablespoons freshly ground pepper
2 tablespoons dried oregano
1 cup (8 fl oz/250 ml) fresh
 lemon juice
salt to taste
4 large flank steaks, about 1½ lb
 (750 g) each

*T*o make the chimichurri sauce, combine all the ingredients in a medium bowl; cover and set aside for up to 5 hours. Makes about 2½ cups (20 fl oz/625 ml).

Grilled Steaks with Chimichurri Sauce;
Latin American Potato Salad;
Tomatoes with Avocado Salsa

❧ To prepare the steaks, place the onions, garlic, chili powder, cumin, pepper, oregano and lemon juice in a blender or food processor and purée; season with salt. Place the steaks in a large glass or plastic container and pour the purée over the meat. Cover and marinate for 2 hours at room temperature or refrigerate overnight.

❧ Prepare a fire in a grill. Position the oiled grill rack 4–6 inches (10–15 cm) above the fire.

❧ When the coals are hot, grill the steaks, turning once, until cooked to your liking, about 3 minutes on each side for rare and 4 minutes on each side for medium rare. Slice the steaks across the grain and serve with the sauce.

TOMATOES WITH AVOCADO SALSA

SERVES 12

This all-purpose salsa is also good with grilled meat, poultry or fish, or spooned inside quesadillas (recipe on page 169).

3 avocados
8 plum tomatoes or 4 regular tomatoes, peeled, seeded and diced
1 tablespoon minced seeded jalapeño (hot green) chili pepper
¼ cup (2 oz/60 g) minced green bell pepper (capsicum)
¼ cup (2 fl oz/60 ml) fresh lemon juice
2 tablespoons red wine vinegar
½ cup (4 fl oz/125 ml) olive oil
2 tablespoons chopped cilantro (fresh coriander)
salt and freshly ground pepper to taste
6 large, firm ripe beefsteak tomatoes

*C*ut the avocados in half, remove the pits and scoop from the shell with a large spoon. Finely dice the avocados.

In a bowl, combine the avocados, diced tomatoes, jalapeño, bell pepper, lemon juice, vinegar, oil and cilantro. Season with salt and pepper and refrigerate for up to 2 hours.

❧ Slice the beefsteak tomatoes and arrange the slices on a platter or individual plates; spoon the avocado salsa over the slices.

LATIN AMERICAN POTATO SALAD

SERVES 12

Potatoes originated in Peru, where this robust salad finds its inspiration. The tangy feta resembles Peruvian queso fresco.

36 small red or white new potatoes (depending on size), about 4 lb (2 kg)
1 cup (5 oz/155 g) minced red (Spanish) onions
1 cup (3 oz/90 g) minced green (spring) onions
3 red or green bell peppers (capsicums), stemmed, seeded, deribbed and diced
6 minced seeded jalapeño (hot green) chili peppers
4 cloves garlic, minced
8 anchovy fillets, minced fine, about 1 tablespoon
¾ cup (6 fl oz/185 ml) red wine vinegar
1 cup (8 fl oz/250 ml) olive oil
2 cups (10 oz/315 g) coarsely crumbled feta cheese
6 hard-cooked eggs, cut into quarters
¼ cup (⅜ oz/10 g) minced cilantro (fresh coriander)
black olives, such as Kalamata or niçoise, for garnish

*P*lace the potatoes in a large saucepan and cover them with cold salted water. Bring to a boil, then reduce heat and simmer, uncovered, until they are cooked through but still firm, about 12–18 minutes, depending on the size of the potatoes. Drain immediately and refrigerate to stop further cooking.

❧ When the potatoes are cool, cut them into halves or quarters. Combine the potatoes, onions and bell peppers in a large bowl and set aside. Combine the jalapeños, garlic and anchovies in a medium bowl or large mortar. Using the back of a large spoon or a pestle, mash this mixture to a paste with some of the vinegar. Add the rest of the vinegar, then whisk in the olive oil. Toss the potatoes, peppers and onions with this vinaigrette. Gently fold in the feta cheese and hard-cooked eggs. Cover and refrigerate for up to 3 hours. Serve garnished with the minced cilantro and olives.

*P*lace tropical fruits directly on the table for a carefree centerpiece.

GRILLED PEPPERED BANANAS WITH BACON

SERVES 12

Warm and sweet, this side dish soothes the palate between bites of spicy food. Try wrapping and grilling fresh pineapple spears, too. If using bamboo skewers, be sure to soak them in warm water for at least 20 minutes first.

6 bananas
freshly ground pepper to taste
12 strips bacon

Prepare a fire in a grill. Position the oiled grill rack 4–6 inches (10–15 cm) above the fire.

Peel the bananas and cut them in half crosswise. Sprinkle each half with pepper and wrap in a piece of bacon. Thread 1 banana half on each of 12 skewers. When the coals are medium-hot, place the bananas on the grill and cook, turning as needed, until the bacon is crisp and the bananas are lightly browned, about 5 minutes.

GRILLED CORN ON THE COB WITH CHILI-LIME BUTTER

SERVES 12

The hint of citrus and chili highlights the corn's natural sweetness. Serve with extra lime wedges to squeeze over the corn.

12 ears corn
¾ cup (6 oz/180 g) unsalted butter at
   room temperature
2 tablespoons chili powder
½ teaspoon cayenne pepper
1 teaspoon paprika
grated zest of 2 limes
¼ cup (2 fl oz/60 ml) fresh lime juice

Remove the husks from the corn. In a bowl, mix the butter, chili powder, cayenne, paprika, lime zest and juice. Spread 1 tablespoon of butter on each ear of corn, then wrap each ear in a large piece of aluminum foil. Refrigerate for up to 3 hours.

Prepare a fire in a grill. Position the oiled grill rack 4–6 inches (10–15 cm) above the fire. When the coals are hot, place the corn on the grill and cook, turning once or twice with tongs, for 10 minutes. Remove the foil before serving.

CAIPIRINHA (RUM & LIME CREAM) PIE

MAKES TWO 9-INCH (23-CM) PIES

This tangy-creamy dessert gets its name from the national Brazilian cocktail.

Basic pie pastry for a double-crust pie
   shell (recipe on page 177)
2 tablespoons (2 envelopes) unflavored
   gelatin dissolved in 1 cup (8 fl oz/
   250 ml) fresh lime juice
1 cup (8 fl oz/250 ml) dark rum
12 egg yolks
2 cups (1 lb/500 g) sugar
grated zest of 4 limes
4 cups (32 fl oz/1 l) heavy (double) cream
1½ cups (5 oz/155 g) toasted flaked
   coconut (see glossary)

Divide the pastry in half. Roll out both halves and use to line two 9-inch (23-cm) pie pans; flute the rims. Set aside in the freezer for 30 minutes or overnight. Fully bake the pie shells as directed on page 177. Cool completely before filling.

Warm the dissolved gelatin and rum in a small saucepan. In a large bowl, beat the egg yolks, gradually adding the sugar, until the mixture is very thick and pale. Fold the gelatin mixture and zest into the yolks. Beat the cream until stiff and fold it into the yolks. Chill the filling until it begins to set, about 30 minutes.

Divide the filling equally between the cooked pie shells, then refrigerate until set completely, about 1½ hours. Top each pie with toasted coconut and serve.

Grilled Peppered Bananas with Bacon, Grilled Corn on the Cob with Chili-Lime Butter (above); Caipirinha (Rum & Lime Cream) Pie (at right)

$\mathcal{J}$NDIAN SUMMER BRUNCH

THERE IS A SPECIAL POIGNANCY to those few weeks in autumn when summer's warmth comes rushing back, calling us outdoors once again. This is an ideal time of year for casual weekend brunches to celebrate birthdays or anniversaries, sports events, or a visit from out-of-town guests.

We set our brunch on a deck framed by trees, but a terrace, a garden or a breakfast nook is fine. Indian summer suggested a color scheme of deep reds, russets and warm golds for table decorations; bright sunflowers and bowls of small lady apples brought this to life. The comforting nature of the recipes inspired the use of homespun touches such as a patchwork quilt for a tablecloth, milk served in an old-fashioned dairy bottle and cloth napkins knotted around miniature rolling pins. The arrival of a friend's puppy happily completed the scene.

A bowl of small apples displayed on the dining table captures the hues of Indian summer.

Menu

To ECHO THE VIBRANT CONTRASTS of this time of year, this menu combines familiar break-fast dishes with exotic North African flavors. Much of the preparation can be done in advance, allowing you to enjoy the morning along with your guests. The choice of dishes allows a leisurely pace of eating.

For the easiest service, start the meal with individual plates of salad on the table along with baskets of toast and jars of marmalade. The eggs can be served directly from the bak-ing dish (nestled in a basket for comfortable handling), followed by the pancakes. Offer a range of hot and cold beverages, including pitchers of sparkling-wine-and-orange-juice mimosas, pots of coffee flavored with cinnamon or cardamom and tea with cinnamon or mint.

Casually knot cotton napkins around a simple host or hostess gift such as a toy rolling pin.

North African Orange Salad

*Baked Eggs, Merguez Sausage,
Peppers & Tomatoes*

Toast

Herbed Lemon Marmalade

*Moroccan Pancakes
with Almond Cream*

WINE RECOMMENDATIONS

Coffee, tea or mimosas may be sipped throughout
the meal. But, if you like, with the salad you could
also pour a light Riesling or an Italian Moscato
d' Asti. That wine could be continued with the
eggs, or you could switch to a brut Champagne
or sparkling wine with a significant amount of
Chardonnay in the blend.

PREPARATION LIST

◆ At least 2 weeks before the brunch, make
the marmalade (or use purchased marmalade).

◆ The night before, prepare and refrigerate
the almond cream; make and refrigerate the
sausage and pepper mixtures for the eggs.

◆ About 30 minutes before serving the salad,
prepare the pancake batter.

◆ After serving the eggs, cook and top
the pancakes.

EACH RECIPE YIELDS 6 SERVINGS.

*In place of quiet music on the stereo, let the
breeze provide the party's score, gently ringing bells
or chimes suspended from a nearby tree.*

NORTH AFRICAN ORANGE SALAD

SERVES 6

Sweet and savory, this orange and olive salad is a nice foil to the spicy egg dish that follows. In winter, try making it with blood oranges.

6 regular oranges or blood oranges
18 Moroccan olives or cured black olives
3 bunches watercress
½ teaspoon ground cinnamon
2 tablespoons confectioners' (icing) sugar
¼ cup (2 fl oz/60 ml) olive oil
3 tablespoons fresh lemon juice
pinch of salt
½ teaspoon ground cumin

Grate the zest of 1 of the oranges and set aside. Remove the peel and pith of all the oranges and cut between the membranes to release all the segments. Remove all seeds. If the oranges are small, simply slice the oranges into rounds and remove the seeds.

Cut the olives in half and remove the pits, or leave them whole. Trim the tough stems from the watercress.

Combine the cinnamon and confectioners' sugar in a shaker, or use a small wire sieve. In a large bowl, combine the oil, lemon juice, salt, cumin and grated zest. Add the watercress and olives and toss well; divide among 6 plates. Top with the orange slices or segments. Sprinkle the oranges with the cinnamon sugar.

North African Orange Salad

BAKED EGGS, MERGUEZ SAUSAGE, PEPPERS & TOMATOES

SERVES 6

Easily assembled, this baked egg dish, known in Tunisia as chakchouka, *features North African–style fresh sausage patties and a pepper-tomato medley.*

FOR THE MERGUEZ:
1 lb (500 g) ground lamb or beef, not too lean
2 cloves garlic, minced
½ teaspoon ground cinnamon
¼–½ teaspoon cayenne pepper, or to taste
1 teaspoon ground cumin
1 tablespoon sweet Hungarian paprika
1 teaspoon ground coriander
1½ teaspoons salt
½ teaspoon freshly ground pepper
2 tablespoons water

FOR THE SAUCE:
3 tablespoons olive oil
2 onions, coarsely chopped
2 cloves garlic, minced
3 large green or red bell peppers (capsicums), stemmed, seeded, deribbed and coarsely chopped
4 large tomatoes, peeled, seeded and chopped
¼ cup (⅜ oz/10 g) chopped cilantro (fresh coriander) and/or parsley
salt and freshly ground pepper to taste

FOR ASSEMBLY:
1 tablespoon olive oil
merguez patties, above
sauce, above
12 eggs

To make the merguez, combine the lamb, garlic, cinnamon, cayenne, cumin, paprika, coriander, salt, pepper and water in a food processor. Pulse to

Baked Eggs, Merguez Sausage, Peppers & Tomatoes; Herbed Lemon Marmalade (page 78)

combine. Form into 12 oval patties; cover and refrigerate for up to 8 hours.
❧ To make the sauce, heat the oil in a large sauté pan. Add the onions and cook over moderate heat until soft, about 10 minutes. Add the garlic and peppers and cook until soft, about 5 minutes. Then add the tomatoes and cook until the tomatoes have melted down, about 10

minutes longer. Stir in the cilantro and/or parsley and season with salt and pepper. Cover and refrigerate for up to 8 hours.
❧ To assemble, preheat an oven to 400°F (200°C). Heat the oil in a heavy frying pan over high heat. Brown the merguez patties on both sides. Remove from the skillet and drain on paper towels. Spoon the sauce into a large

baking dish. Arrange the merguez patties around the perimeter, then break the eggs into the center. Or, divide the sauce among 6 small gratin dishes, place 2 merguez patties in each gratin dish, then break 2 eggs into each one. Bake until the whites are set but the yolks are still soft, about 20 minutes for the large dish, about 8–10 minutes for individual gratins.

HERBED LEMON MARMALADE

MAKES 8 CUPS (64 OZ/2 KG)

Fresh mint and mint tea combine with lemon verbena and orange flower water to perfume this preserve. Let the marmalade rest for 2 weeks before serving.

4 lb (2 kg) large, juicy lemons,
    about 10–12
10 cups (2½ qt/2.5 l) cold water
4 mint tea bags
8 cups (4 lb/2 kg) sugar
3 tablespoons orange flower water,
    optional
32 whole mint leaves
16 lemon verbena leaves, optional

Wash and dry the lemons. Remove the zest with a vegetable peeler, being careful not to remove any pith; cut zest into very thin strips and place in a saucepan, cover with about 1 cup (8 fl oz/250 ml) of the water and bring to a boil. Cook for 2 minutes, then discard the water. Cover with 1 more cup (8 fl oz/250 ml) of the water and soak the zest overnight.

&❧ Cut the peeled lemons in half crosswise and slice as thinly as possible. Remove the seeds. Put the sliced lemons in a large, heavy enameled or stainless-steel pot. Cover with the remaining 8 cups (64 fl oz/2 l) water and let soak overnight.

&❧ The next day, bring the lemons to a boil with the mint tea bags and simmer, uncovered, for 15 minutes. Let sit for 3 hours, then remove and discard the tea bags. Add the soaked zest and sugar and bring to a boil. Simmer, uncovered, until a small spoonful of the mixture gels slightly on a chilled plate, about 35 minutes. Stir in the optional orange flower water. Place 2 mint leaves and

1 optional lemon verbena leaf in the bottom of each of 8 hot sterilized 1-cup (8-fl oz/250-ml) canning jars. Pour in the marmalade, leaving ½ inch (12 mm) of head space, top with the remaining leaves, then seal the jars. Process in a hot-water bath for 10 minutes (see Canning, page 186), or store in the refrigerator for up to 3 months. *(Pictured on previous page.)*

MOROCCAN PANCAKES WITH ALMOND CREAM

SERVES 6

These yeast-leavened pancakes are more substantial than most Western pancakes.

FOR THE ALMOND CREAM:
4 cups (32 fl oz/1 l) milk
¾ cup (3 oz/90 g) ground toasted
    almonds (see glossary)
¾ cup (6 oz/185 g) sugar
¼ cup (1 oz/30 g) cornstarch (cornflour)
4 egg yolks
1 teaspoon vanilla extract (essence)
½ teaspoon almond extract (essence)
2 tablespoons orange flower water

FOR THE PANCAKES:
1 tablespoon active dry yeast
1 teaspoon sugar
¼ cup (2 fl oz/60 ml) warm
    (110°F/43°C) water
1½ cups (7½ oz/235 g) all-purpose
    (plain) flour
¼ teaspoon salt
¼ teaspoon ground cinnamon
1 egg
1¼ cups (10 fl oz/300 ml) milk

TO COOK AND SERVE:
oil for cooking
6 small bananas
¾ cup (3 oz/90 g) toasted whole
    or slivered almonds (see glossary)
julienne strips of orange zest, optional

To prepare the almond cream, combine the milk, the almonds and half of the sugar in a medium saucepan. Place over moderate heat and bring to scalding. Remove from heat, cover the pan and let steep for 30 minutes. Strain, pressing down on the almonds with the back of a spoon to release the most flavor possible. Reheat the milk. In a small bowl, combine the cornstarch, remaining sugar and egg yolks; beat in a small amount of the warm milk. Pour this mixture back into the pan and cook, stirring, over moderate heat until the mixture thickens and boils for 1–2 minutes. Remove from the heat and stir in the extracts and the orange flower water. Let cool, then cover and refrigerate for up to 8 hours.

&❧ To make the pancakes, combine the yeast, sugar and warm water in a small bowl. Set aside in a warm place until foamy, about 10 minutes. Sift the flour, salt and cinnamon together into a medium bowl. Make a well in the center and add the yeast mixture. In a small bowl, beat together the egg and milk. Stir gradually into the flour and yeast mixture until a smooth batter is formed. Cover the bowl and let the mixture rise in a warm place for 1 hour.

&❧ Brush a griddle with oil, heat until very hot, then lower the heat to moderate. Drop heaping tablespoonfuls of batter on the griddle. Cook until bubbles appear. Turn the pancakes over and cook until golden brown, about 1 minute longer. Transfer to baking sheets, but do not stack. Keep warm in a low oven.

&❧ Slice the bananas and fold them into the almond cream. Spoon over the warm pancakes and top with the toasted almonds and, if desired, the orange zest. Serve at once.

Moroccan Pancakes with Almond Cream

PHOTOGRAPH BY PETER JOHNSON

HARVEST LUNCH

IN VINEYARDS AND ON FARMS everywhere, family, friends and co-workers stop harvesting at midday to share a simple feast that highlights nature's bounty. We chose a vineyard location for our harvest lunch, but you don't need to live or work in the countryside to enjoy this autumnal celebration. Whether you set your table beneath trees, on a patio or near a sunny window, what matters is an abundance of seasonal food and a spirit of fellowship.

We aimed to capture the feel of the harvest by using a rustic, weather-beaten table, setting it with ceramic dishes and simple cutlery. For the centerpiece, we gathered wild-flowers from a nearby garden; any mixed seasonal blooms from a flower vendor do just as well. Fresh fruit or grape clusters, bunches of autumn leaves and vine trimmings are also fitting tokens of the harvest to add to your decorations.

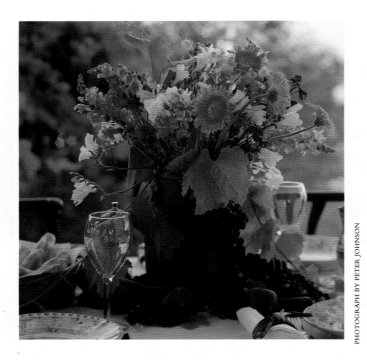

PHOTOGRAPH BY PETER JOHNSON

Wildflowers and vine trimmings are casually arranged in a large vase or pitcher to form the centerpiece.

Menu

THE MENU THAT FOLLOWS features seasonal fare that's abundant, yet simple to prepare. While the ingredients are readily available in food stores, the best fruits and vegetables—especially figs and blue plums—will probably be found at your local farmer's market. And be sure to take advantage of this occasion to offer one or more of your favorite vintage or varietal wines.

This menu doesn't have to be limited by the seasons, however. With the substitutions suggested in the recipe introductions, you'll find that these dishes can be reliable standbys at lunches and dinners throughout the year.

A watering can becomes an impromptu vase for seasonal blossoms for a side table. Clusters of just-picked grapes, hung by their stems from the side of the can or draped alongside it, are an edible embellishment.

PHOTOGRAPH BY PETER JOHNSON

*Grilled Peppered Figs
with Grilled Goat Cheese in Grape Leaves*

Walnut Focaccia

❧

*Butterflied Leg of Lamb
in Middle Eastern Yogurt Marinade*

Spiced Apricot Chutney

*Grilled Eggplant
with Sweet Cherry Tomato Sauce*

Lentil Salad

❧

Blue Plum Tart

PREPARATION LIST

◆ Several months ahead, prepare the chutney (commercial chutney may be substituted).

◆ Up to 1 week ahead, make the cherry tomato sauce for the eggplant.

◆ The day before, wrap and oil the cheese.

◆ The night before, marinate the lamb.

◆ The morning of the lunch, bake the focaccia; make the lentil salad and the plum tart.

◆ One hour before, let the lamb come to room temperature before grilling.

EACH RECIPE YIELDS 6 SERVINGS.

Bottles of a favorite vintage, adorned with flowers and homemade name tags, make ideal gifts for guests.

PHOTOGRAPH BY PETER JOHNSON

WINE RECOMMENDATIONS

Celebrate the harvest with a choice of flavorful young white and red wines. Choose a white with generous flavor and fruit that echoes the menu's sweet-sour contrasts: a rich Chardonnay from Australia or America or a dry Gewürztraminer. The red wine should be full-bodied, but not heady: a fresh Pinot Noir or a Cabernet blend. With dessert, offer chilled plum brandy.

GRILLED PEPPERED FIGS WITH GRILLED GOAT CHEESE IN GRAPE LEAVES

SERVES 6

The sweetest figs of all are often the cracked, homely looking ones. When figs are not in season, substitute peaches or good, juicy pears.

six 1-inch-thick (2.5-cm) slices mild
   fresh goat cheese
6 bottled grape leaves, rinsed of brine
   and stemmed
6 large ripe figs
6 thin slices prosciutto
olive oil for brushing
freshly ground pepper to taste
6 lime wedges

Wrap each slice of goat cheese in a grape leaf, folding in the ends and sides so it resembles a neat packet. If made ahead, cover and refrigerate overnight.
❧ Prepare a fire in a grill. Position the oiled rack 4–6 inches (10–15 cm) above the fire. Or, preheat a broiler (griller).
❧ Cut each fig in half lengthwise. Cut the prosciutto slices in half lengthwise. Wrap each fig half with a piece of prosciutto and thread 2 halves on each of 6 skewers. Brush the wrapped figs and cheese lightly with olive oil and sprinkle with pepper.
❧ Cook the figs and cheese on the grill over medium-hot coals or broil until figs are heated through (about 3 minutes) and the cheese is soft and warm (about 4 minutes), turning once. Divide the figs and cheese among 6 small plates and garnish each with a lime wedge.

WALNUT FOCACCIA

MAKES ONE 11- BY 18-INCH
(28- BY 46-CM) FOCACCIA

Add grapes to this hearty bread if you are not serving the figs in the same menu. Toasted walnut oil is richer in flavor than pale, untoasted varieties.

FOR THE DOUGH:
2 teaspoons active dry yeast
1¼ cups (10 fl oz/300 ml) warm
   (110°F/43°C) water
2 tablespoons sugar
3¾ cups (19 oz/595 g) unbleached
   all-purpose (plain) flour
3 tablespoons toasted walnut oil
1 teaspoon salt

FOR THE TOPPING:
toasted walnut oil
1 cup (4 oz/125 g) chopped toasted
   walnuts (see glossary)
2 tablespoons minced fresh rosemary
2 cups (10 oz/315 g) halved and seeded
   red grapes, optional
1–2 tablespoons sugar, optional

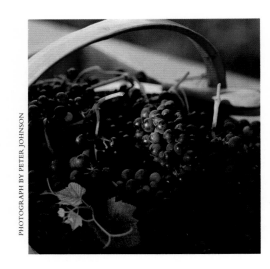

PHOTOGRAPH BY PETER JOHNSON

Newly harvested grapes, cut from the vines with a traditional knife, wait in a wooden lug to go to the winepress.

To make the dough, dissolve the yeast in ½ cup (8 fl oz/250 ml) of the warm water in the bowl of an electric mixer. Add the sugar and ½ cup (2½ oz/75 g) of the flour and mix to combine. Cover and let sit for about 30 minutes. Add the remaining flour, the remaining water, the walnut oil and the salt and mix well. Beat on low speed with the dough hook attached until the dough leaves the bowl cleanly, about 10 minutes. Or, mix the dough in a food processor until well combined. Then turn out onto a lightly floured board and knead until the dough is smooth and elastic, about 10 minutes, adding more flour if necessary to prevent sticking. Transfer the dough to an oiled bowl, cover with a kitchen towel and let rise in a warm place until doubled, about 1 hour.
❧ Preheat an oven to 475°F (240°C). Punch down the dough and turn it out on a lightly floured board. Form into an 11- by 18-inch (28- by 46-cm) rectangle and place in a sided baking pan of the same dimensions. Cover the dough loosely and allow it to rest until doubled, about 15–30 minutes.
❧ To make the topping, brush the dough lightly with walnut oil, then dimple the top with your fingers. Sprinkle with the walnuts and rosemary. (If using grapes, push them into the dough and sprinkle the focaccia with the sugar, then add the walnuts and rosemary.) Bake on the lower rack of the oven until golden brown on top, about 12–15 minutes.

Grilled Peppered Figs with Grilled Goat Cheese in Grape Leaves; Walnut Focaccia

BUTTERFLIED LEG OF LAMB IN MIDDLE EASTERN YOGURT MARINADE

SERVES 6

A butterflied leg of lamb has thick and thin portions, yielding both rare and medium meat. The very simple marinade produces spectacular results.

1 large leg of lamb, about 6 lb (3 kg), boned, butterflied and trimmed of fat and silverskin
1 large onion, chopped
2–3 cloves garlic, minced
½ teaspoon ground cinnamon
½ teaspoon ground cardamom
¼ teaspoon saffron threads, crushed
1 teaspoon ground ginger or 1 tablespoon grated fresh ginger
1 tablespoon ground coriander
½ teaspoon freshly ground pepper
2 cups (1 lb/500 g) plain lowfat or nonfat yogurt
3 tablespoons fresh lemon juice
½ cup (¾ oz/20 g) chopped fresh mint
oil for brushing
salt and freshly ground pepper to taste

*P*lace the butterflied lamb leg in a glass or plastic container large enough to hold it in one layer. Set aside.
❧ Place the onion and garlic in a food processor or blender and pulse until coarsely chopped. Add the cinnamon, cardamom, saffron, ginger, coriander, pepper, yogurt, lemon juice and mint and purée. Pour over the lamb, cover and marinate overnight in the refrigerator, turning occasionally.

Butterflied Leg of Lamb in Middle Eastern Yogurt Marinade; Spiced Apricot Chutney; Grilled Eggplant with Sweet Cherry Tomato Sauce

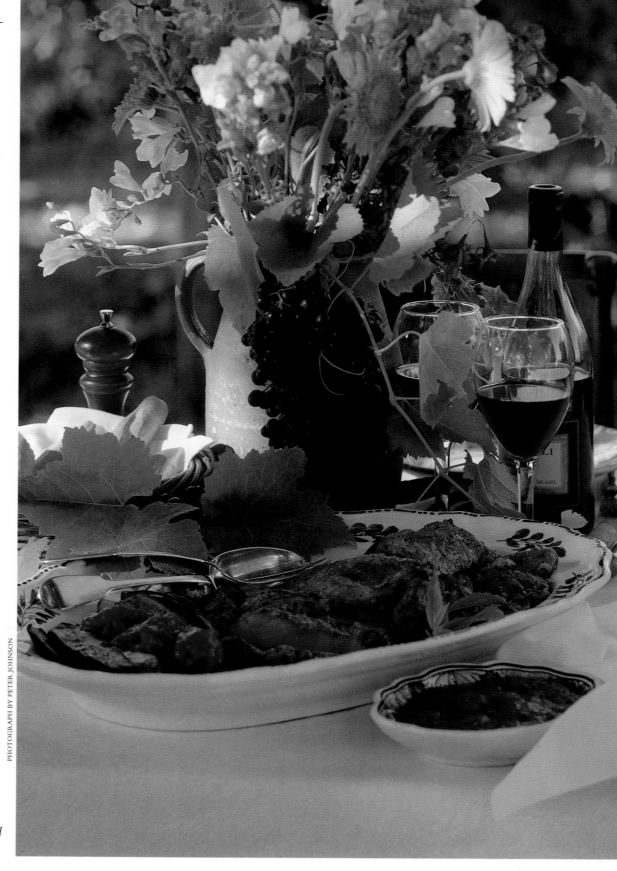

PHOTOGRAPH BY PETER JOHNSON

❧ Prepare a fire in a grill. Position the oiled rack 4–6 inches (10–15 cm) above the fire. Or, preheat a broiler (griller).

❧ Remove the lamb from the marinade. Brush with oil and sprinkle with salt and pepper. Grill over medium-hot coals or broil for 8–10 minutes on each side for rare, or 12 minutes for medium rare. The thicker section may take a few minutes longer. Slice across the grain to serve.

SPICED APRICOT CHUTNEY

MAKES ABOUT 6 CUPS (48 OZ/1.5 KG)

Sweet-tart apricots have an affinity for lamb. Make the chutney when the fruit is in season and let it sit in a cool, dark place for 2–3 weeks to mellow the flavors before using. Or, substitute commercial chutney.

6 cups (1½ lb/750 g) pitted and
    quartered fresh apricots
2 cups (1 lb/500 g) sugar
½ tablespoon salt
1 onion, chopped
one 4- by 1½-inch (10- by 4-cm)
    piece fresh ginger, peeled and sliced
3 cloves garlic
1 teaspoon ground cinnamon
½ teaspoon ground cloves
½ teaspoon cayenne pepper or 3–4
    jalapeño (hot green) chili peppers,
    minced
1½ cups (12 fl oz/375 ml)
    cider vinegar

*P*lace the apricots in a large, heavy enameled or stainless-steel pot. Cover with the sugar and salt and let stand for at least 1 hour or up to 8 hours.

❧ In a food processor or blender, pulse or blend the onion, ginger, garlic, cinnamon, cloves and cayenne or chilies until chopped. Add half of the vinegar and purée. Pour this mixture over the apricots and stir in the remaining vinegar. Bring to a boil, then reduce heat and simmer, uncovered and stirring often, until the mixture is thick and a teaspoonful sets up on a chilled plate, about 1 hour. Pour into 3 hot sterilized 2-cup (16-fl oz/500-ml) canning jars, leaving about ½ inch (12 mm) of head space, then seal the jars. Process in a hot-water bath for 10 minutes (see Canning, page 186) or store in the refrigerator for up to 3 months.

GRILLED EGGPLANT WITH SWEET CHERRY TOMATO SAUCE

SERVES 6

The sauce, more like a conserve, is also excellent on cream cheese, goat cheese or grilled chicken.

FOR THE CHERRY TOMATO SAUCE:

2 cups (12 oz/375 g) stemmed
    cherry tomatoes
½ cup (3½ oz/105 g) light brown
    sugar, packed
grated zest of 1 lemon
¼ cup (2 fl oz/60 ml) fresh
    lemon juice
1 tablespoon grated fresh ginger
3 tablespoons water
½ teaspoon ground cinnamon
½ teaspoon ground cumin
pinch of cayenne pepper
salt and freshly ground pepper to taste

FOR THE GRILLED EGGPLANT:

1 clove garlic, crushed
¼ cup (2 fl oz/60 ml) olive oil,
    slightly warmed
2 firm globe eggplants (aubergines),
    about ½–¾ lb (250–375 g) each, or
    6 slender (Asian) eggplants (aubergines)
salt and freshly ground pepper to taste

*T*o make the sauce, combine the tomatoes, brown sugar, lemon zest, lemon juice, ginger, water, cinnamon, cumin and cayenne in a saucepan. Cook, uncovered, over moderate heat, stirring occasionally, until the tomatoes break down and the mixture becomes thick and syrupy, about 30 minutes. Season with salt and pepper and transfer to a bowl or jar. If desired, cover and refrigerate up to 1 week. Makes about 1 cup (8 fl oz/250 ml).

❧ To make the grilled eggplant, steep the garlic in the warm olive oil for about 1 hour. Prepare a fire in a grill. Position the oiled rack 4–6 inches (10–15 cm) above the fire. Or, preheat a broiler (griller). Peel the globe eggplants and slice them 1 inch thick (2.5 cm) crosswise. If using slender eggplants, do not peel; cut each in half lengthwise and score the top with the point of a knife. Brush the eggplants with the garlic oil and sprinkle with salt and pepper. Grill or broil the eggplant, turning once, until soft but not too browned, about 3 minutes on each side.

❧ Meanwhile, rewarm the tomato sauce over low heat. When the eggplants are done, divide the slices among 6 plates (or place 2 halves of slender eggplant on each), top with the tomato sauce and serve.

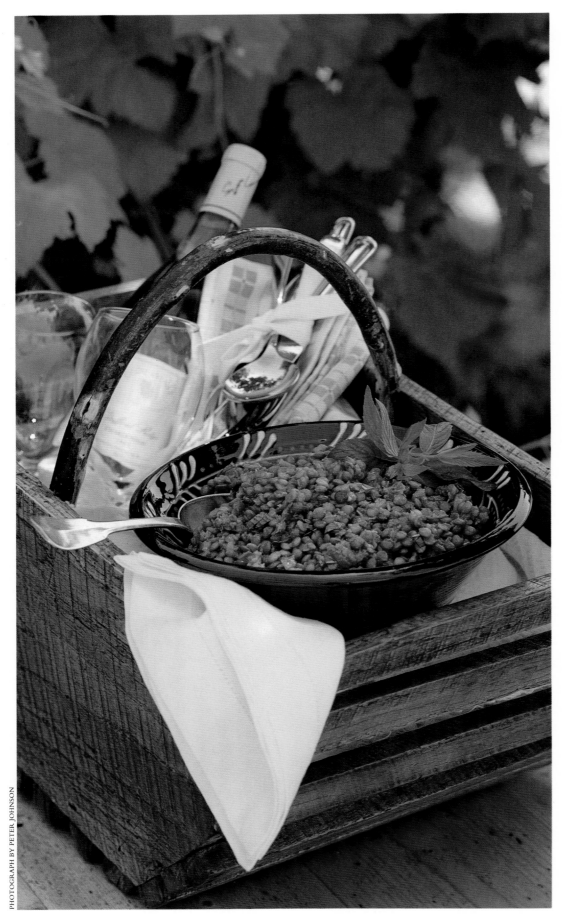

Lentil Salad

LENTIL SALAD

SERVES 6

For the best texture, make the salad no more than several hours in advance. If you make it ahead, fold in half the mint, adding the rest before serving.

2 cups (14 oz/440 g) green or
   brown lentils
1 bay leaf
1 teaspoon salt
½ cup (4 fl oz/125 ml) plus 3 tablespoons olive oil
¼ cup (2 fl oz/60 ml) fresh
   lemon juice
2 cups (8 oz/250 g) diced onions
1 teaspoon minced garlic
2 tablespoons ground cumin
1 teaspoon ground coriander
grated zest of 1 lemon
½ cup (¾ oz/20 g) chopped
   fresh mint
salt and freshly ground pepper to taste

*P*lace the lentils and bay leaf in a deep saucepan and cover with cold water to a depth of 3 inches (7.5 cm) above the lentils. Bring to a boil over high heat, add the salt, reduce heat and simmer, covered, until the lentils are tender but still firm. Green lentils can take as long as 45 minutes, brown as few as 15, so keep testing. When the lentils are done, drain off any excess water, toss the lentils in the ½ cup (4 fl oz/125 ml) olive oil and the lemon juice and set aside.

Heat the remaining 3 tablespoons oil in a large sauté pan, add the onions and cook until tender and translucent, about 10 minutes. Add the garlic, cumin, coriander and lemon zest and cook 2–3 minutes longer. Add the cooked onion mixture to the lentils. Fold in the mint and season with salt and pepper. Serve at room temperature.

PHOTOGRAPH BY PETER JOHNSON

Blue Plum Tart

BLUE PLUM TART

MAKES ONE 8- BY 11-INCH (20- BY 28-CM)
RECTANGULAR TART OR ONE 10-INCH
(25-CM) ROUND TART

*Plum and citrus flavors predominate in
this nutty tart. Substitute other varieties
of plums for the prune plums if necessary.*

basic pie pastry for a single-crust pie
  shell (recipe on page 177)
½ cup (2 oz/60 g) plus 2 tablespoons
  hazelnuts, toasted and skinned
  (see glossary)
½ cup (4 oz/125 g) plus 2
  tablespoons sugar
½ teaspoon ground cinnamon
½ teaspoon ground ginger
3 tablespoons unsalted butter at
  room temperature

16–20 Italian prune plums, halved
  and pitted
¾ cup (6 fl oz/180 ml) orange
  marmalade
whipped cream flavored with about 1
  teaspoon grated orange zest, optional

Preheat an oven to 400°F (200°C).
Roll out the pastry into a large rectangle
on a lightly floured surface. Use to
line an 8- by 11-inch (20- by 28-cm)
rectangular tart pan or a 10-inch
(25-cm) round tart pan. Set aside in the
freezer while you make the filling.
❧ Finely chop the ½ cup (2 oz/60 g)
hazelnuts and coarsely chop the remaining 2 tablespoons hazelnuts. Combine
the finely chopped hazelnuts, the ½ cup
(4 oz/125 g) sugar, cinnamon, ginger
and butter in a food processor or a

medium bowl; pulse or cut in the butter
with a pastry cutter or 2 knives until
blended into a paste. Press onto the
bottom of the pastry-lined tart pan. Top
with the plums, arranged in overlapping
rows. Sprinkle with the remaining 2
tablespoons sugar and bake on the middle
rack of the oven for 10 minutes. Reduce
the heat to 350°F (180°C) and bake
until the plums are bubbly and the crust
is golden, about 20–30 minutes more.
❧ Meanwhile, melt the orange marmalade in a small saucepan; strain and keep
warm. When the tart is done, brush the
marmalade over the plums and sprinkle
with the 2 tablespoons coarsely chopped
hazelnuts. If desired, serve each piece
with a dollop of orange-flavored
whipped cream.

$\mathcal{P}$RE-THEATER COCKTAILS

WHEN GROUPS OF FRIENDS gather together to attend an evening event such as a play, opera or dance performance, dinner can pose a challenge. With curtain-up usually between 7 and 8 P.M., there is little time for a sit-down meal. That's why a cocktail party makes such perfect sense, not just before a show but for any occasion when you want to entertain guests without extending the party into a full night's event.

We set our cocktail party in a living room with a lovely city view, but a den or library anywhere is also appropriate. Because of the relaxed style of this gathering, we decorated the room simply by placing seasonal foliage and fruit in various spots. The owner's collection of personal memorabilia served as the ideal backdrop.

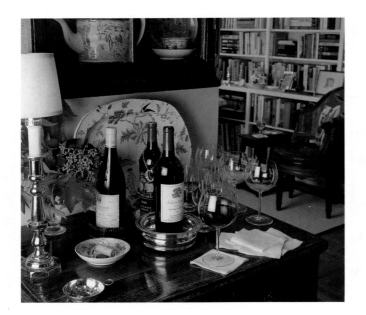

On a side table, an arrangement of wine bottles, glasses and cocktail napkins allows guests to serve themselves.

THE ARRAY OF FINGER FOODS and small dishes selected for this cocktail party for twelve offers something to please everyone. The portions are generous enough to keep appetites at bay all evening. Autumn flavors predominate, since fall is the time when many arts seasons begin, but you can make these recipes any time of year. Most dishes can be prepared at least partly in advance, with minimal cleanup.

Try placing platters of food with plenty of small plates, cutlery and cocktail napkins at various convenient spots around the room where guests can serve themselves. Likewise, you might want to arrange separate stations for a self-service wine bar and a full liquor bar with ready-to-mix cocktails and mineral water. In so doing, you'll establish different conversation areas and encourage guests to mingle.

Menu

Seasonal foliage and fruits, such as autumn leaves and persimmons, add a simple, elegant decorative flourish.

TOMATO TART

MAKES 12 SERVINGS

Similar to a quiche, this French-style tart could be given an Italian flair by substituting basil for the mint and mozzarella for the Gruyère.

basic pie pastry for a single-crust pie
    shell (recipe on page 177)
3 large tomatoes, cut into ½-inch-
    thick (12-mm) slices
salt to taste
2 tablespoons Dijon mustard
3 tablespoons chopped fresh mint
4 oz (125 g) Gruyère or Emmenthaler
    cheese, cut into 8 thin slices
2 eggs
1 cup (8 fl oz/250 ml) heavy
    (double) cream
freshly ground pepper to taste

℞oll out the pastry and use it to line a 10-inch (25-cm) pie or tart pan. Set it aside in the freezer for 30 minutes.
℘ With your fingers, carefully push out the seeds and watery juices from the tomato slices. Sprinkle the sliced tomatoes with salt and place in a large colander to drain. After 30 minutes, remove the tomatoes from the colander and pat them dry.
℘ Preheat an oven to 350°F (180°C). With a rubber spatula, spread the mustard over the bottom of the tart shell and sprinkle the chopped mint over the mustard. Top with the cheese, then place the tomato slices over the cheese. In a small bowl, beat together the eggs and cream, season with salt and pepper and pour over the tomatoes. Bake until pale gold and the custard is set, about 30 minutes. Let rest for 10 minutes, then slice and serve.

Tomato Tart; Roasted Eggplant Salad

ROASTED EGGPLANT SALAD

MAKES 12 SERVINGS

If you make this low-fat salad ahead of time, wait until just before serving to fold in the mint and almonds.

3 large globe eggplants (aubergines)
1 cup (8 oz/250 g) plain nonfat yogurt
2 tablespoons fresh lemon juice or
    to taste
1 tablespoon minced garlic
1 teaspoon minced jalapeño (hot green)
    chili pepper or more to taste
2 teaspoons ground cumin
salt and freshly ground pepper to taste
⅔ cup (3 oz/90 g) toasted almonds
    (see glossary), chopped
¼ cup (⅜ oz/10 g) chopped fresh mint
4 pita bread rounds, cut into 6
    wedges each

℘reheat an oven to 400°F (200°C). Place the eggplants on a baking sheet and prick all over with a fork. Roast, turning occasionally for even cooking, until the eggplants are soft and tender, about 1 hour. Remove from the oven and let sit until cool enough to handle. Peel the eggplant and place the pulp in a colander to drain for about 30 minutes.
℘ Place the eggplant pulp in a food processor or blender and pulse to purée. Add the yogurt, lemon juice, garlic, jalapeño and cumin. Pulse quickly to mix. Add salt and pepper. Transfer the purée to a serving bowl. If desired, cover and refrigerate for up to 6 hours. Stir in the chopped toasted almonds and mint and serve with the pita wedges.

CRAB SALAD IN ENDIVE LEAVES

MAKES 24 APPETIZERS

The crisp, slightly bitter endive contrasts nicely with the mild sweetness of the crab. Substitute small romaine leaves if you like.

grated zest of 1 lemon
2 tablespoons lemon juice
1 teaspoon chopped fresh tarragon
2 tablespoons chopped fresh chives
2 tablespoons chopped fresh parsley
1 tablespoon Dijon mustard
½ cup (4 fl oz/125 ml) mayonnaise or
  as needed to bind
1 lb (500 g) fresh crab meat, picked
  over and any cartilage removed
¾ cup (4 oz/125 g) diced celery
salt, freshly ground pepper and cayenne
  pepper to taste
24 Belgian endive (chicory/witloof) leaves

*I*n a bowl, combine the lemon zest, lemon juice, tarragon, chives, parsley, mustard and mayonnaise; mix well. Stir in the crab and celery and season with salt, ground pepper and cayenne. Cover and refrigerate up to 6 hours. To serve, spoon the crab mixture into the endive leaves and chill for at least 30 minutes or up to 2 hours to firm the filling.

A slice of tomato tart, a glass of wine and an inviting chair await a guest.

BAKED CLAMS OREGANATI

MAKES 36 APPETIZERS

When preparing live clams, tap each one to be sure the shells close tightly.

36 Manila or littleneck clams, scrubbed
dry white wine
3 tablespoons olive oil
2 cloves garlic, minced
1 tablespoon dried oregano
½ cup (2 oz/60 g) dried bread crumbs
1 tablespoon chopped fresh parsley
3 tablespoons freshly grated Parmesan
  cheese, optional
salt and freshly ground pepper to taste
rock salt
lemon wedges

*P*lace the clams in a large sauté pan with about 1 inch (2.5 cm) of white wine. Cover the pan and steam over high heat just until the clams open, 2–8 minutes. Remove from the heat immediately and, using a slotted spoon, transfer the clams to a platter; discard any unopened clams. Remove the top shells and discard. Loosen each clam from its bottom shell with a knife so that it can be picked up easily. Strain the juices in the pan and reserve.
❧ Warm the olive oil in a small sauté pan, add the garlic and oregano and cook over low heat for 2 minutes. Remove from the heat and stir in the bread crumbs, parsley and Parmesan, if desired. Let cool. Sprinkle the bread crumbs over the clams and drizzle with a few drops of the reserved pan juices. Season with salt and pepper. Cover and refrigerate until serving time.
❧ To serve, preheat a broiler (griller). Arrange the clams on a rock salt–lined baking pan that can fit under the broiler. Broil the clams until browned on top, about 5 minutes. Serve with lemons.

MUSHROOMS STUFFED WITH SWEET SAUSAGE

MAKES 24 APPETIZERS

You can stuff and refrigerate the mushroom caps the morning of the party.

24 large fresh mushrooms
4 tablespoons (2 fl oz/60 ml) oil
½ cup (2 oz/60 g) chopped onion
1 tablespoon minced garlic
½ lb (250 g) ground pork
½ teaspoon ground cinnamon
¼ teaspoon ground nutmeg
1 teaspoon toasted fennel seed, ground
  (see glossary)
1 tablespoon grated orange zest
¼ cup (1 oz/30 g) dried bread crumbs
salt and freshly ground pepper to taste
1 cup (8 fl oz/250 ml) chicken stock

*R*emove the stems from the mushrooms and chop them; reserve the caps. Heat 2 tablespoons of the oil in a large sauté pan. Add the chopped onion and cook until soft, about 5 minutes. Add the chopped stems and cook over high heat until they start to become dry, about 5 minutes. Stir in the garlic and cook for 1 minute. Transfer to a bowl and set the mixture aside.
❧ Heat the remaining 2 tablespoons of oil in the same pan. Cook the pork, breaking it up with a fork, until it is no longer pink, about 5 minutes. Stir in the cinnamon, nutmeg, fennel seed and orange zest. Add the cooked mushroom and onion mixture and the bread crumbs; mix well. Season with salt and pepper and adjust the rest of the spices.
❧ Preheat the oven to 350°F (180°C). Stuff the pork mixture into the mushroom caps. Place the mushrooms in a baking pan and drizzle the stock around them. Bake until cooked through, about 20–25 minutes. Serve warm.

Baked Clams Oreganati; Mushrooms Stuffed with Sweet Sausage; Crab Salad in Endive Leaves

MEDITERRANEAN EASTER

EASTER IS A JOYOUS HOLIDAY in the Mediterranean, where it is usually celebrated with a midday or evening feast laden with symbols of the birth of a new season. Crisp greens, fresh seafood, tender spring lamb, fragrant herbs, plump eggplants and artichokes, sweet honey and rich nuts and cheese—each is a gift from the reawakening earth and each finds its way onto the Mediterranean Easter table.

For our holiday meal, we chose the dining room of a charming home with views of the surrounding hillsides. We set the table with handmade glazed pottery to complement the earthy food. To bring springtime sights and scents indoors, we decorated the room with bundles and bouquets of herbs and terra-cotta pots of fresh oregano, thyme and rosemary. Look for these in vegetable shops, farmer's markets and garden nurseries.

Small pots of Mediterranean herbs surround a place setting with fragrances of the new season.

YOU DON'T HAVE TO OBSERVE the holiday to enjoy this Easter repast; it requires only a desire to celebrate the season. The food for this meal is perfect for family-style serving, with everything passed informally on platters at the table. Accompanying wines may be placed on a nearby sideboard, ready to open and share as the meal progresses.

For a traditional Easter symbol, try dyeing eggs using a natural, old-fashioned method. First, bring yellow onion skins to a boil in a saucepan of water to make a russet-colored dye; let the liquid cool. Then, form a pattern on the egg shells with thin strips of masking tape. Dip the eggs into the dye and let them dry on a rack before peeling off the tape to reveal the pattern. Or display small, mottled quail eggs, found in specialty food shops.

Menu

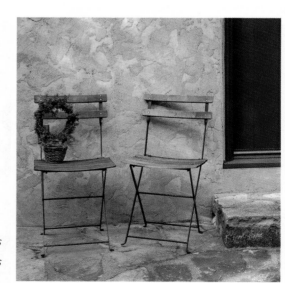

On a side patio, two rustic chairs could provide a couple of guests with a quiet spot for conversation.

Gypsy Spinach Pie

Salmon Dolmas with Avgolemono

*Rack of Spring Lamb Marinated in
Garlic, Allspice, Cumin & Thyme*

*Artichoke Hearts with
Tomatoes & Currants*

Stuffed Eggplant

*Asparagus & Potatoes
with Almonds & Mint*

*Citrus & Honey Cheesecake
with Nut Crust*

PREPARATION LIST

◆ Up to 2 days ahead, start marinating the lamb.

◆ The day before, make the artichokes and the egg-plant; re-warm the artichokes on the stovetop and the eggplant in the oven just before serving.

◆ The morning of the party, bake the cheesecake.

◆ Up to 4 hours ahead, make the spinach pie; roast the potatoes and blanch the asparagus.

◆ Two to 3 hours in advance, assemble the dolmas; bake them and prepare the sauce just before serving.

EACH RECIPE YIELDS 6 SERVINGS AND CAN
EASILY BE DOUBLED TO SERVE 12 AS SHOWN.

*Early strawberries add their sweet blush to
glasses of Spanish sherry.*

WINE RECOMMENDATIONS

With the spinach pie, serve a Sauvignon Blanc from Chile, France or California, or a moderately rich Italian Soave. With the salmon, pour a dry Chenin Blanc or a Washington State Riesling. For the lamb, offer a hearty, rich Italian red such as Barolo, or an American Merlot. With dessert, a Spanish cream or brown sherry.

GYPSY SPINACH PIE

MAKES ONE 9-INCH (23-CM) PIE (6 SERVINGS)

This robust two-crust pie also makes a nice lunch on its own. To serve twelve, make two pies as shown.

basic pie pastry for a double-crust pie
    shell (recipe on page 177)
2 lb (1 kg) spinach (about 4 bunches),
    washed well and stemmed; or a
    mixture of spinach, beet (beetroot)
    greens, sorrel and Swiss chard
    (silverbeet), about 8–9 cups; or two
    10-oz (315 g) packages frozen
    chopped spinach, thawed
¼ cup (2 oz/60 g) unsalted butter or
    olive oil (2 fl oz/60 ml)
2 bunches green (spring) onions, chopped
2 tablespoons all-purpose (plain) flour
salt and pepper to taste
¼ teaspoon ground nutmeg, or
    to taste
⅛ teaspoon cayenne pepper
¼ cup (1 oz/30 g) toasted pine nuts
    (see glossary)
½ cup (3 oz/90 g) dried currants,
    soaked in warm water for 10 minutes
½ cup (¾ oz/20 g) chopped
    fresh parsley
½ cup (¾ oz/20 g) chopped
    fresh dill
4 hard-cooked eggs
¼ cup (1 oz/30 g) toasted bread crumbs
olive oil for brushing

*P*reheat an oven to 375°F (190°C).
Roll out the pastry for the bottom crust
and use it to line a 9-inch (23-cm) pie
pan. Roll out the pastry for the top
crust and set it aside.

❧ Place the spinach or greens with the
water clinging to the leaves in a large
frying pan and stir over medium heat

Gypsy Spinach Pie

until wilted, about 3 minutes. Drain well, chop coarsely and squeeze as dry as possible.

❧ Heat the butter or oil in a small sauté pan. Add the green onions and cook until soft, about 3 minutes. Stir in the flour and cook 2–3 minutes longer. Add this mixture to the chopped greens and season well with salt, pepper, nutmeg and cayenne. Fold in the pine nuts, drained currants, parsley and dill. Slice the hard-cooked eggs.

❧ Sprinkle the bread crumbs in a layer in the bottom of the pastry-lined pie pan, then add the greens mixture. Top with the sliced eggs. Brush the edge of the bottom crust with water, place the top crust on the pie and trim the excess dough, then crimp the edges together. Cut a steam hole in the center of the top crust and decorate the top with the pastry trimmings. Brush the crust top with olive oil and bake on the middle rack of the oven until golden, about 40 minutes. Remove from the oven and let rest for 10 minutes before slicing.

SALMON DOLMAS WITH AVGOLEMONO

SERVES 6

In traditional dolmas, a rice filling is wrapped in the grape leaves and fresh lemon juice is squeezed over the top.

1⅛ lb (560 g) salmon fillet, skinned
12 bottled grape leaves, rinsed of brine and stemmed
1 cup (8 fl oz/250 ml) fish stock or chicken stock
2 eggs, separated
2 tablespoons fresh lemon juice
freshly ground pepper to taste
chopped fresh dill
lemon wedges

Preheat an oven to 450°F (230°C). Cut the salmon into twelve 1½-oz (45-g) strips, each about 2½ inches (6 cm) long and 1½ inches (4 cm) wide. Wrap each piece in a grape leaf. Place the dolmas seam-side down in a shallow baking pan. Drizzle the fish stock or chicken stock over the dolmas and bake until the fish is firm but not mushy, about 4–5 minutes.

❧ Meanwhile, in a bowl, beat the egg yolks and lemon juice together until frothy. In a separate bowl, beat the egg whites until soft peaks form and fold them into the yolks.

❧ Remove the dolmas to warm individual plates. Pour the stock into a small sauté pan. Add the egg mixture to the warm stock, whisking constantly until thickened, 1–2 minutes. Pour the sauce over the dolmas, sprinkle with pepper and the chopped dill and serve at once, garnished with lemon wedges.

Salmon Dolmas with Avgolemono

Rack of Spring Lamb Marinated in Garlic, Allspice, Cumin & Thyme; Stuffed Eggplant; Artichoke Hearts with Tomatoes & Currants; Asparagus & Potatoes with Almonds & Mint (page 108)

RACK OF SPRING LAMB MARINATED IN GARLIC, ALLSPICE, CUMIN & THYME

SERVES 6

The marinade combines Greek, Turkish and North African flavors. For twelve guests, double the recipe as shown.

FOR THE MARINADE:

1 onion, grated

2 tablespoons minced garlic

3 tablespoons fresh lemon juice

grated zest of 1 lemon and 1 orange

1 tablespoon Dijon mustard

1 teaspoon ground allspice

2 teaspoons ground cumin

½ teaspoon cayenne pepper

2 tablespoons chopped fresh thyme
   leaves, or 2 teaspoons dried thyme

1 teaspoon freshly ground pepper

½ cup (4 fl oz/125 ml) olive oil

FOR THE LAMB:

2 racks of lamb, trimmed, or 12
   lamb chops

oil for brushing chops

salt to taste for chops

*T*o make the marinade, combine the onion, garlic, lemon juice, lemon zest, orange zest, mustard, allspice, cumin, cayenne, thyme and ground pepper in a food processor or blender. Pulse or blend to purée. Gradually add the olive oil until the mixture is blended.

❧ Place the lamb in a glass or plastic container and coat the meat with the marinade. Cover and refrigerate for at least 6 hours or up to 2 days.

❧ To cook the racks, preheat an oven to 350°F (180°C). Sear the racks in a cast-iron frying pan over high heat or on a hot griddle until browned on all sides, then transfer to a roasting pan and roast in the oven until a meat thermometer inserted in the center of a rack reads 125°F (52°C), about 10–12 minutes. Let the lamb rest for 10 minutes on a carving board, covered with aluminum foil, before slicing; meat will be medium rare.

❧ To cook the chops instead, preheat a broiler (griller). Or, prepare a fire in a grill and position the oiled grill rack 4–6 inches (10–15 cm) above the fire. Brush the chops with oil, sprinkle with salt and broil or grill them for 3 minutes on each side for rare, or 4 minutes on each side for medium rare.

ARTICHOKE HEARTS WITH TOMATOES & CURRANTS

SERVES 6

Sweet-sour artichoke preparations such as this one are common in the Mediterranean.

6 large (about 4-inch/10-cm diameter) artichokes
1 lemon half
2 tablespoons fresh lemon juice
¼ cup (2 fl oz/60 ml) olive oil
1 cup (8 fl oz/250 ml) water, stock or dry white wine
2 cups (12 oz/375 g) peeled, diced tomatoes or drained and chopped canned plum tomatoes
½ cup (3 oz/90 g) dried currants, soaked in warm water to cover for 10 minutes
2 tablespoons honey
salt and freshly ground pepper to taste

*C*ut the stems and tops off of the artichokes, break off and discard most of the outer leaves and remove all the rest with a sharp knife. Scoop out the fuzzy chokes with a small sharp spoon. Rub the cut surfaces with the lemon half and float the artichoke hearts in a bowl of cold water mixed with the lemon juice until all the artichokes

are prepared. Drain and pat dry just before cooking.

❧ Pour the olive oil into a large sauté pan and place over medium-high heat. Add the artichoke hearts and toss them to coat with the oil and add the water, stock or wine. Cover the pan and steam until the artichoke hearts are tender-crisp, about 12–15 minutes (most of the liquid will have been absorbed). Add the tomatoes, drained currants and honey; stir well and simmer, uncovered, until the artichokes are tender when pierced with a knife and the pan juices have reduced, about 10 minutes longer. Season with salt and pepper and add more honey or lemon juice if desired. Transfer the artichoke hearts to a platter and spoon the sauce on top.

STUFFED EGGPLANT

SERVES 6

Be sure to precook the eggplant shells to make them tender and completely edible.

3 baby globe eggplants (aubergines) or 6 slender (Asian) eggplants (aubergines)
salt
½ cup (4 fl oz/125 ml) plus 2 tablespoons olive oil
1 large onion, chopped
4 large cloves garlic, minced
1 tablespoon dried oregano
1½ cups (9 oz/280 g) peeled, diced tomatoes
¼ cup (⅜ oz/10 g) chopped fresh parsley
freshly ground pepper to taste
½ cup (4 fl oz/125 ml) water

*C*ut the eggplants in half lengthwise. With a sharp knife, carefully score the flesh and remove most of the eggplant pulp, leaving a shell that is ¼ inch (6 mm) thick. Dice the pulp and set aside. Salt the eggplant shells and let sit,

flesh sides down, in a colander for 1 hour, then rinse and pat dry.

❧ Preheat an oven to 350°F (180°C). Warm 2 tablespoons of the olive oil in a large sauté pan. Add the onion and cook until tender and translucent, about 10 minutes. Set aside in a bowl. In the same pan, heat 6 tablespoons (3 fl oz/90 ml) of the olive oil, add the diced eggplant and cook until softened, about 5 minutes. Stir in the garlic, oregano and tomatoes and simmer for about 3 minutes. Add the onion and parsley to this mixture. Season to taste with salt and pepper and set aside.

❧ Heat the remaining 2 tablespoons of the oil in a large sauté pan and cook the eggplant shells, turning once or twice, for a few minutes to soften them. Then place them side by side in an oiled baking dish and stuff with the reserved filling. Add the water to the pan, cover and bake until very tender, about 45 minutes.

*P*lant a selection of Mediterranean herbs in terra-cotta pots. They make beautiful table displays and the leaves can be used in myriad recipes.

Speckled quail eggs, home-dyed hens' eggs and globes of bay leaves connote Easter's earthly splendors. To make the herb globes, attach bay laurel or other leaves to a Styrofoam ball with a hot-glue gun. If desired, gird each sphere with wire for extra holding.

ASPARAGUS & POTATOES WITH ALMONDS & MINT

SERVES 6

In this quickly assembled vegetable combination, pine nuts would also go well with the mint and fresh basil with the almonds.

24 small new red potatoes (about 3 lb/ 1.5 kg)
about 2 tablespoons olive oil for coating plus ¼ cup (2 fl oz/60 ml)
.salt and freshly ground pepper to taste
2 lb (1 kg) fresh asparagus
1 cup (8 fl oz/250 ml) chicken stock
2 cloves garlic, minced
½ cup (2 oz/60 g) toasted sliced or slivered almonds (see glossary)
½ cup (¾ oz/20 g) chopped fresh mint or basil

Preheat an oven to 400°F (200°C). Place the potatoes in a baking pan, coat them with about 2 tablespoons of the olive oil and sprinkle with salt and pepper. Roast until the potatoes are cooked through but firm, about 25–35 minutes depending on size. Remove from the oven and let sit until cool enough to handle.

❧ Meanwhile, prepare the asparagus. Snap off the tough end of each stalk. If the stalks are thick, peel the bottom 2–3 inches (5–7.5 cm) with a vegetable peeler. Bring about 2 inches (5 cm) of salted water to a boil in a frying pan. Lay the asparagus in the pan and cook until tender-crisp, 3–5 minutes. Remove the asparagus and plunge them into ice water, then drain and pat dry. Cut the asparagus into 2-inch (5-cm) lengths.

❧ Cut the cooled potatoes into quarters. Warm the ¼ cup (2 fl oz/60 ml) olive oil in a very large sauté pan. Add the potatoes and heat them through. Add the asparagus, chicken stock and garlic and simmer a few minutes to heat through. Season with salt and pepper, then add the almonds and mint or basil and serve.

Asparagus & Potatoes with Almonds & Mint

CITRUS & HONEY CHEESECAKE WITH NUT CRUST

MAKES ONE 9-INCH (23-CM) CHEESECAKE

Use dark honey for a fuller-bodied, more intense flavor. The cheesecake is best served slightly warm or at room temperature.

FOR THE CRUST:

2 cups (8 oz/250 g) hazelnuts, toasted and skinned (see glossary)

⅓ cup (3 oz/90 g) sugar

½ teaspoon ground cinnamon

4–5 tablespoons (2–2½ oz/60–80 g) unsalted butter, melted

FOR THE CHEESE FILLING:

1½ lb (750 g) cream cheese at room temperature

½ cup (4 fl oz/125 ml) sour cream at room temperature

¾ cup (9 oz/280 g) full-flavored honey

6 eggs, separated, at room temperature

1 tablespoon grated lemon zest

1 tablespoon grated orange zest

1 teaspoon vanilla extract (essence)

3 tablespoons chopped candied orange peel, optional

¼ cup (2 oz/60 g) sugar

FOR THE GARNISH:

chopped toasted and skinned hazelnuts (see glossary)

fresh strawberries, optional

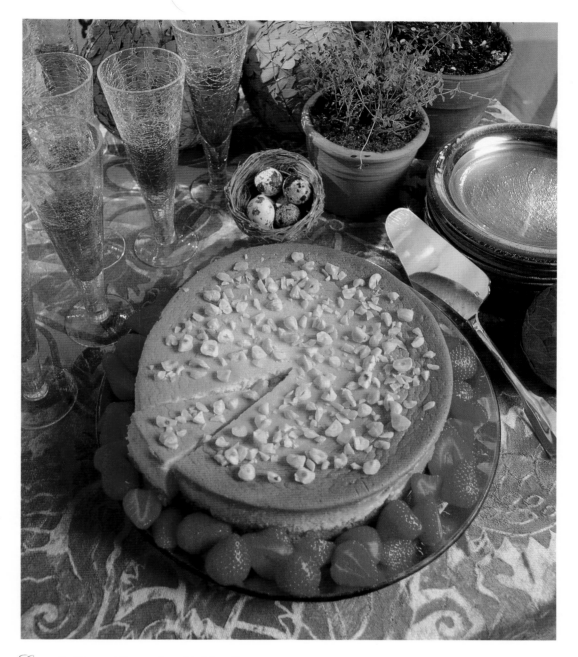

Citrus & Honey Cheesecake with Nut Crust

To make the crust, chop the nuts with the sugar and cinnamon in a food processor as finely as possible; do not let it turn to paste. Add enough butter for the mixture to hold together. Press this mixture into the bottom and partially up the sides of a 9-inch (23-cm) spring-form pan. Set aside.

❧ To make the filling, preheat an oven to 350°F (180°C). Place the cream cheese and sour cream in the bowl of an electric mixer. Beat until smooth with the paddle attachment or beaters. Add the honey and beat until there are no lumps. Add the egg yolks, lemon and orange zests, vanilla and, if using, candied orange peel; mix well.

❧ In a large bowl, beat the egg whites until frothy. Gradually beat in the sugar until the peaks are almost stiff. Stir one third of the egg whites into the cheese mixture, then fold in the rest. Pour into the prepared cake pan. Bake on the middle rack of the oven until set just on the edges, about 45–50 minutes; gently shake the pan to test. Turn off the oven and leave the cheesecake inside with the door ajar for 2 hours.

❧ Remove the sides from the pan and slide the cheesecake onto a plate. Top with chopped hazelnuts and, if desired, arrange berries around the cheesecake.

TRADITIONAL THANKSGIVING

A MERICAN FAMILIES EVERYWHERE hold the national harvest celebration dear to their hearts. The Thanksgiving feast provides some of our most enduring holiday memories and features a roster of ingredients so ritualized that they have become almost sacred.

We presented our Thanksgiving menu in a classic American dining room featuring an extra-long table so it could accommodate not only the guests but also the roast turkey. Side dishes and other courses were placed close at hand on a sideboard. We also set up a separate children's table, a tradition in some families. Heirloom dishes and antique silver, glassware and linens were selected to reinforce a sense of family heritage. Wreaths, baskets, nuts, dried corn, wheat sheaves and game bird feathers helped to evoke the spirit of the American harvest.

As our holiday menu shows, there is room for creativity within the traditional bounds of the Thanksgiving meal. Here butternut squash takes over for pumpkin in the first-course soup, while a vivid tangerine custard assumes the pumpkin's usual role as a pie filling. The turkey features a corn bread stuffing enriched with sweet Italian sausage and subtle spices perfume the cranberry sauce.

It takes advance planning to cook and serve such an extensive menu. We recommend that you carefully read through the preparation list and the recipes up to several weeks before Thanksgiving Day, allowing yourself ample time for shopping and advance cooking. By all means, mix and match this menu with your own favorites as you wish.

Keep place settings uncomplicated. Set the soup plate atop the dinner plate and provide only essential cutlery and glasses.

Menu

WINE RECOMMENDATIONS

The first choice to accompany Thanksgiving turkey is a just-released Beaujolais Nouveau. For white wine drinkers, pour a Riesling from Germany's Rhine or Mosel regions. With dessert, offer a late-harvest Semillon from Australia or America, or an outstanding Sauternes.

Spiced Squash & Apple Soup

❧

*Roast Turkey
with Corn Bread Stuffing*

Cranberry Chutney

*Chanterelles, Chestnuts &
Pearl Onions with Thyme*

Celery Root & Potato Purée

Brussels Sprouts with Garlic & Parmesan

❧

Tangerine Custard Tart

*A wooden cupboard opens to reveal a collection of glistening
Early American silver pieces for coffee and tea service.*

PREPARATION LIST

◆ Up to 1 week ahead, make the chutney.

◆ Up to 2 days ahead, make and refrigerate the
tangerine custard pie filling.

◆ The day before, make the soup; prepare
the stuffing (but do not stuff the turkey).

◆ On Thanksgiving morning, prepare and bake
the pie crust.

◆ Three hours before, fill and top the pie.

◆ Up to several hours ahead, prepare the celery
root and potato purée.

◆ Fifteen minutes before, bake the chanterelle
casserole; start cooking the Brussels sprouts.

EACH RECIPE YIELDS 12 SERVINGS.

*Baskets and bowls of nuts, dried Native
American corn and sheaves of wheat are
strong symbols of Thanksgiving's blessings.*

Along with the soup, serve basketfuls of bakery breads. Loaves with raised decorations in the forms of wheat, hearts and leaves are especially homey.

SPICED SQUASH & APPLE SOUP

SERVES 12

Butternut squash is similar to pumpkin in taste and texture but is easier to peel and dice. Apple lightens and sweetens the purée.

4 tablespoons (2 oz/60 g) unsalted
   butter or olive oil
2 large onions, diced, about 4 cups
   (1¼ lb/625 g)
2 large green apples, peeled, cored and
   diced, about 2 cups (1 lb/500 g)
1 teaspoon ground nutmeg
½ teaspoon ground allspice
½ teaspoon ground cinnamon
10 cups (5 lb/2.4 kg) peeled and diced
   butternut squash (about 4 whole)
12 cups (3 qt/3 l) chicken stock
salt and freshly ground pepper to taste
thin slices of green apple for garnish

*M*elt the butter or heat the olive oil in a large pot over moderate heat. Add the diced onions and apples and cook until tender, about 10 minutes. Stir in the spices, cook for 1 minute, then add the squash and chicken stock. Bring to a boil, reduce the heat and simmer, uncovered, until the squash is very tender, about 20–30 minutes.
ह Purée the vegetables in batches with a little bit of the stock in a blender or food processor. Transfer to a large bowl. Add enough of the remaining stock to make a medium-thick soup. Reserve any leftover stock if not serving right away, as the soup may thicken on standing. Season with salt and pepper and adjust the spices. This soup may be made a day ahead, refrigerated uncovered until cold and then covered.
ह To serve, in a large pot heat the soup almost to scalding. Ladle into bowls and top with thin slices of apple.

Spiced Squash & Apple Soup

ROAST TURKEY WITH CORN BREAD STUFFING

SERVES 12

While the turkey roasts, make the giblet stock; just before carving, use the stock to make the gravy. For best results, always use fresh (not frozen) turkey.

FOR THE STUFFING:

2 tablespoons olive oil
1 lb (500 g) sweet Italian sausages, removed from casings and crumbled
6 tablespoons (3 oz/90 g) unsalted butter
2 onions, diced, about 1½ cups (8 oz/250 g)
1 cup (5 oz/155 g) diced celery
2 cloves garlic, minced
2 tablespoons finely chopped fresh marjoram or sage
2 teaspoons ground fennel seed
½ teaspoon ground nutmeg
½ teaspoon ground cinnamon
1 cup (8 fl oz/250 ml) chicken stock
4 cups (8 oz/250 g) packaged corn bread stuffing
salt and freshly ground pepper to taste

FOR THE TURKEY:

1 fresh turkey, 12–14 lb (6–7 kg), neck and giblets removed for gravy
1 lemon, cut in half
1 clove garlic
salt, freshly ground pepper and sweet paprika to taste

FOR THE GIBLET STOCK AND GRAVY:

turkey neck and giblets
8 cups (64 fl oz/2 l) water or chicken stock
2 sliced onions
2 sliced peeled carrots
1 or 2 celery ribs
1 fresh thyme sprig
1 clove garlic
2 tablespoons all-purpose (plain) flour
salt, freshly ground pepper and ground allspice to taste

To prepare the stuffing, heat the oil in a large sauté pan. Add the sausage and sauté until browned. Remove from the pan with a slotted spoon and set aside. Add the butter to the pan and cook the onions until translucent, about 10 minutes. Add the celery, garlic, marjoram or sage, fennel seed, nutmeg, cinnamon and the stock and cook 3 minutes longer. Transfer to a large bowl and add the sausage and corn bread. Season with salt and pepper and mix well. At this point, you can cover and refrigerate the stuffing overnight.

❧ To prepare the turkey, preheat an oven to 350°F (180°C). Wipe the turkey with a damp cloth and rub the body cavity with the cut lemon and garlic and salt. Sprinkle the outside with salt, pepper and paprika.

❧ Spoon the stuffing loosely into the body and neck cavities and sew or truss them closed. Place any extra stuffing in a buttered casserole, moisten with a little extra stock and cover. Place in the oven 1 hour before the turkey is done.

❧ To roast the turkey, place it breast-side down on a rack in a roasting pan. Tent with aluminum foil. Roast for 20 minutes per pound (4–4½ hours total). Uncover the turkey and turn it breast-side up for the last 45 minutes of baking.

❧ Meanwhile, to prepare the giblet stock, simmer the neck, gizzard and heart (do not use the liver) in a large pan with the water or stock, onions, carrots, celery, thyme and garlic. Bring to a boil, then reduce heat and simmer for 1½ hours, skimming the surface; add more stock as needed. Remove the neck and discard. Remove the giblets and chop fine. Discard the thyme. Transfer the cooked vegetables with a slotted spoon to a blender and purée. Reserve the giblets, giblet stock and the puréed vegetables to make the gravy.

❧ The turkey is done when a meat thermometer inserted in the thickest part of the thigh (away from the bone) registers 180°F (82°C). Remove from the oven and let rest at least 15 minutes before carving. Remove the stuffing.

❧ To make the gravy, pour off all but 3 tablespoons of drippings from the roasting pan. Place the pan over medium heat and stir in the 2 tablespoons flour until bubbly, then add 1 cup (8 fl oz/250 ml) of the reserved giblet stock. Bring to a boil. Stir in the vegetable purée and thin with additional stock. Add the chopped giblets. Season with salt, pepper and allspice. Carve the turkey (see page 178). Serve with the stuffing and gravy.

CRANBERRY CHUTNEY

MAKES ABOUT 6 CUPS (48 OZ/1.5 KG)

This sweetly spiced variation on traditional cranberry sauce may be made weeks ahead.

2 cups (16 fl oz/500 ml) water
3 cups (1½ lb/750 g) sugar
2 unpeeled oranges, diced, seeded and finely chopped in a blender
two 2-inch (5-cm) pieces fresh ginger, peeled and cut into thin slices
4 cups (1 lb/500 g) cranberries
1 teaspoon ground cinnamon
½ teaspoon ground cloves
1 cup (6 oz/185 g) raisins

Combine the water and sugar in a deep saucepan and bring to a boil, stirring. Add the oranges and ginger; reduce heat and simmer, uncovered, for 20 minutes. Add the cranberries, cinnamon and cloves and cook, uncovered, until thickened, about 15 minutes. Stir in the raisins and cook until big bubbles appear, about 7 minutes. Pour into a bowl and let cool. Serve or cover and refrigerate for up to 1 week.

Roast Turkey with Corn Bread Stuffing; Cranberry Chutney

CHANTERELLES, CHESTNUTS & PEARL ONIONS WITH THYME

SERVES 12

Peeling fresh chestnuts is a painstaking task, but worth every minute of hot-fingered torture. See if you can talk some-one into helping you, as the chestnuts must be hot for the inner skin to come off. Or purchase canned peeled chestnuts instead.

1 lb (500 g) chestnuts
1 lb (500 g) cipolline or pearl onions
2 lb (1 kg) chanterelles or brown
  mushrooms
8 tablespoons (4 oz/125 g) unsalted
  butter
2 tablespoons chopped fresh thyme
½ cup (4 fl oz/125 ml) chicken stock,
  or as needed
salt and freshly ground pepper to taste

Cut a cross in the rounded side of each chestnut. Place in a single layer in one or more large saucepans, cover with water and bring to a boil. Reduce heat and simmer, uncovered, for 10 minutes. While the chestnuts are hot, remove the outer peel and the thin inner brown skin. Try to keep the chestnuts whole, if possible. If the center is whiter than the outside, the chestnuts are not cooked through; simmer them in additional water for about 8–10 minutes more. (The chestnuts are done when the inside is the same color as the cooked outer parts. Cut one in half to check.) Set the cooked chestnuts aside.

❧ Trim the roots of the onions care-fully without cutting across the ends. Cut a cross on the bottom of each onion to prevent them from telescoping while cooking. Place the onions in a medium saucepan, cover with water and bring to a boil. Reduce heat and sim-mer, uncovered, until tender-firm, about 8–10 minutes. Drain, let cool slightly, then remove the peels. Set the onions aside.

❧ Wipe the mushrooms clean with a damp paper towel or clean with a mushroom brush. Cut into thick slices. Or, if the mushrooms are small, leave them whole. Melt half of the butter in a large sauté pan and sauté half of the mushrooms over high heat until soft-ened, 3–5 minutes. Repeat with the remaining butter and mushrooms.

❧ To serve, preheat an oven to 350°F (180°C). Combine the cooked chest-nuts, onions and mushrooms in a large casserole. Toss with the thyme. Add enough chicken stock to moisten the mixture. Season with salt and pepper. Bake until heated through, about 15 minutes. Serve at once.

CELERY ROOT & POTATO PURÉE

SERVES 12

Celery root contributes a subtle edge of sweetness and lightness. It's best to purée the potatoes with a ricer or food mill since processors yield gummy results.

8 large baking potatoes
3 large celeriacs (celery roots)
3–4 cups (24–32 fl oz/750 ml–1 l)
  chicken stock
6 tablespoons (3 oz/90 g) unsalted butter
1 cup (8 fl oz/250 ml) heavy
  (double) cream
salt, freshly ground pepper and ground
  nutmeg to taste

Preheat an oven to 400°F (200°C). Poke the potatoes in several places with a fork and bake until very tender, about 1 hour. Cut in half, remove the pulp and pass it through a ricer or food mill.

❧ While the potatoes are baking, trim the leaves and roots from the celeriacs and peel. Cut into dice and simmer, uncovered, in enough chicken stock to cover until very tender, about 25 minutes. Drain and purée in a food processor or pass through a food mill.

❧ Combine the potato and celeriac purée in a large, heavy saucepan over moderate heat. Stir in the butter and cream; if necessary add more butter and cream or stock until a thick, smooth consistency is achieved. Season with salt, pepper and a little nutmeg.

BRUSSELS SPROUTS WITH GARLIC & PARMESAN

SERVES 12

The sprouts stand up well to the large quantity of garlic in this vivid green, quickly cooked side dish.

3 lb (1.5 kg) Brussels sprouts
¼ cup (2 oz/60 g) unsalted butter
¼ cup (2 fl oz/60 ml) olive oil
12 large cloves garlic, minced
1½–2 cups (12–16 fl oz/375–500 ml)
  chicken stock
salt and freshly ground pepper to taste
1½ cups (6 oz/185 g) freshly grated
  Parmesan cheese

Trim the ends from the Brussels sprouts and cut the sprouts in half lengthwise. Heat the butter and oil in 1 or 2 sauté pans large enough to hold all the Brussels sprouts in one layer. Add the garlic and cook over low heat to remove the bite, about 2 minutes. Add the Brussels sprouts and chicken stock to a depth of 1½ inches (4 cm) and cover the pan. Simmer until tender-crisp, stirring occasionally, about 5–8 minutes. Season with salt and pepper and top with the cheese. Serve at once.

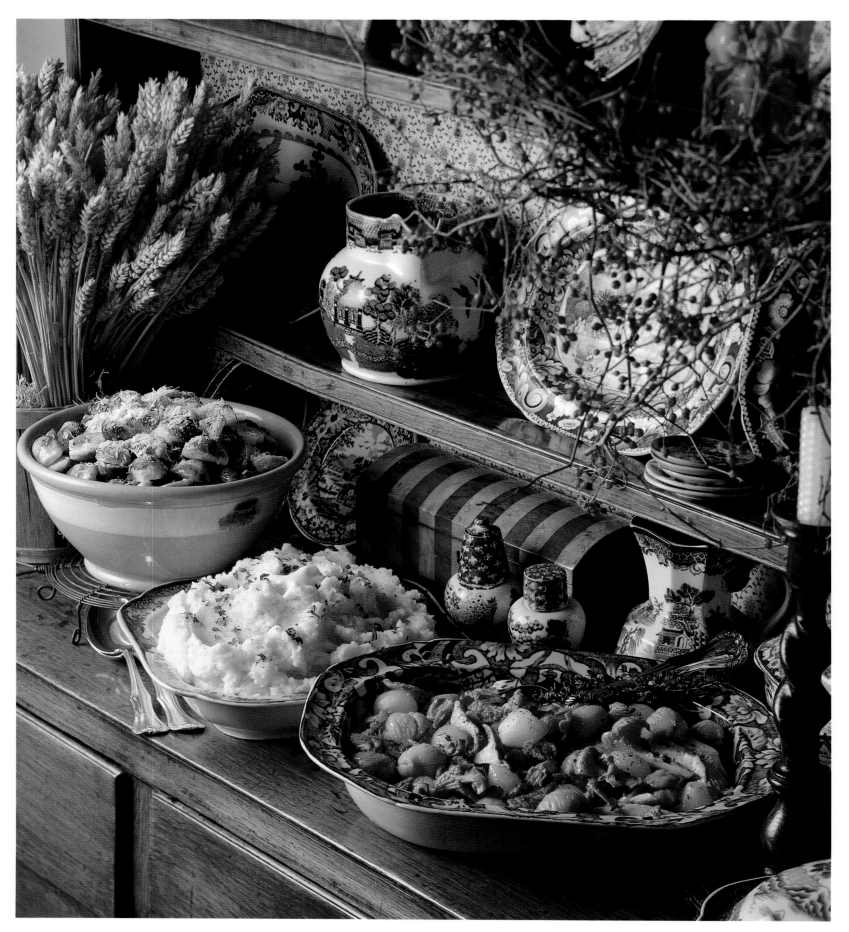

Brussels Sprouts with Garlic & Parmesan; Celery Root & Potato Purée; Chanterelles, Chestnuts & Pearl Onions with Thyme

TANGERINE CUSTARD TART
MAKES TWO 10-INCH (25-CM) TARTS

Sweet-tart tangerines make an elegant curdlike filling for a festive dessert. Be sure to grate the tangerine zest for the topping before you juice the fruit for the filling.

FOR THE TARTS:
12 egg yolks
1 cup (8 fl oz/250 ml) fresh
   tangerine juice
½ cup (4 fl oz/125 ml) fresh
   lemon juice
1½ cups (12 oz/375 g) granulated
   sugar
8 tablespoons (4 oz/125 g) unsalted
   butter, cut into small bits
grated zest of 6 tangerines
2 tablespoons mandarin orange liqueur
basic pie pastry for a double-crust pie
   shell (recipe on page 177)

FOR THE TOPPING:
2 cups (16 fl oz/500 ml) heavy
   (double) cream
¼ cup (1½ oz/45 g) sifted confectioners' (icing) sugar
grated zest of 4 tangerines
mandarin orange liqueur to taste

To make the filling, combine the egg yolks, juices and sugar in a bowl. Strain into a heavy stainless-steel saucepan or the top part of a double boiler set over, but not touching, simmering water and whisk the mixture constantly until thick. Stir in the butter, zest and mandarin orange liqueur. Cover and chill for at least 3 hours or up to 2 days.

☙ Roll out half of the pastry and use it to line a 10-inch (25-cm) tart pan. Repeat with the other half of the pastry. Set the shells aside in the freezer for 30 minutes. Fully bake the pie shells as directed on page 177. Cool completely, then spread equal amounts of tangerine filling in each pie shell.

☙ To make the topping, in a bowl whip the cream until it holds soft peaks; beat in the confectioners' sugar, tangerine zest and mandarin orange liqueur. Spread the cream evenly over the top of each pie, filling almost to the edges.

Decorate the dessert table with fresh tangerines arranged with poetic simplicity in a wooden bowl.

Tangerine Custard Tart

CASUAL HANUKKAH BUFFET

HANUKKAH, THE FESTIVAL OF LIGHTS, commemorates the rededication of the Temple of Jerusalem some 2,100 years ago. For eight successive evenings in November or December, Jewish families light candles to mark that event. Especially on the first and last nights, they gather together to feast and give gifts.

Appropriate for any convivial get-together in late autumn or winter, our Hanukkah party takes place in a large kitchen, where everyone can savor the warmth and rich aromas. If your kitchen is big enough, by all means use it; at the very least, you can set dishes out on the counter for buffet-style service. We lit candles in a traditional Jewish menorah to mark the start of the meal, but any candlelight will add to the ambience. Displays of fruits and nuts are apt decorations to grace the entire kitchen.

The menorah displays one lighted candle for each night of Hanukkah and an additional candle to light the others.

Menu

THIS HEARTY WINTER BUFFET is made up of traditional Eastern European-style dishes that have become as synonymous with Hanukkah as turkey is with Thanksgiving. They belong to the category of comfort foods, excellent for a cold-weather meal any time.

In observation of Jewish dietary laws, we kept the menu free of dairy ingredients. But if you don't keep kosher, feel free to garnish the borscht and latkes with sour cream and the pecan torte with whipped cream.

Once the candles have been lit, you could start the meal by ladling the soup at the table, then ask guests to join you in the kitchen to cook the latkes. Let guests help themselves from the buffet for the main course and dessert.

Everyday items, such as baskets, pitchers, dried wildflowers and pretty containers, adorn a kitchen counter.

Beet, Cabbage & Mushroom Borscht

Potato Latkes

Chunky Applesauce

Spiced Brisket of Beef

Carrot Tsimmes

Pecan Torte

Tangerine Sorbet

PREPARATION LIST

◆ Two to 3 days ahead, coat the brisket with the spices.

◆ Up to 2 days ahead, make and refrigerate the applesauce to be rewarmed before serving.

◆ The day before, prepare the borscht and make and freeze the sorbet.

◆ The morning of the party, make the torte.

◆ Just before dinner, start the potato latkes.

EACH RECIPE YIELDS 6 SERVINGS.

Potted narcissus, a simple basket of pears and softly glowing candles symbolize the winter season in a dramatic still-life composition.

WINE RECOMMENDATIONS

Many high-quality kosher wines are made today in Israel, France, New York and California. Select one red wine for the meal which is light to medium in body and both spicy and earthy in flavor: a supple Cabernet Sauvignon or an herbal Merlot would work well. With dessert, sip a tawny port or a cream sherry.

BEET, CABBAGE & MUSHROOM BORSCHT

SERVES 12

An Eastern European favorite, this tastes best if made the day before. Supplement any leftovers with extra brisket for the next day's meal.

8–10 large beets (beetroots)
3 tablespoons olive oil
2 large red (Spanish) onions, chopped
6 large carrots, peeled and sliced
2 heads cabbage, shredded
4 cups (12 oz/375 g) sliced
  fresh mushrooms

1 lemon, pricked with a fork in
  several places
10 cups (2½ qt/2.5 l) beef or
  vegetable stock
salt and freshly ground pepper to taste
sugar to taste
fresh lemon juice if needed
½ cup (¾ oz/20 g) chopped
  fresh dill

*C*ut the greens from the beets, leaving about 2 inches (5 cm) of stems attached. Wash the beets well, place them in a pot and cover with cold water. Bring to a boil, then reduce the heat and simmer, uncovered, until tender, about 30–50 minutes, depending on the size of the beets. Drain. Cover the beets with lukewarm water. When cool, slip off the skins and dice the beets. Set aside.

In a stockpot, warm the olive oil over moderate heat. Add the onions and carrots and cook for about 10 minutes, stirring occasionally. Add the cabbage, beets, mushrooms, lemon and stock; bring to a boil. Reduce the heat and simmer, uncovered, until the soup is red and the flavors are blended, about 30 minutes. Remove the lemon. Season with salt and pepper; adjust the seasoning with sugar and lemon juice if necessary. Sprinkle with chopped dill before serving.

Beet, Cabbage & Mushroom Borscht

POTATO LATKES

MAKES ABOUT 24 POTATO PANCAKES

Grate the potatoes and onions for more robust potato pancakes; dice and purée them for finer-textured results.

2 small onions
6–7 large russet potatoes, peeled
2 large eggs, beaten
2 teaspoons salt
1 teaspoon freshly ground pepper
¾–1 cup (4–5 oz/125–155 g)
   all-purpose (plain) flour
vegetable shortening or oil for frying

Grate the onions and potatoes and place them in a large bowl. Using paper towels, blot up any liquid they might have released and stir in the eggs, salt, pepper and enough flour to bind the mixture.

❧ Heat 2 inches (5 cm) of melted shortening or oil in a large frying pan and drop in spoonfuls of batter. Cook until golden brown, about 3 minutes on each side. Drain on paper towels and keep warm in a 350°F (180°C) oven while cooking the remaining batter. Serve as soon as the last batch is cooked; latkes will stay crisp for only a few minutes.

❧ Alternately, dice the onions and potatoes. Place half of the diced onions and 1 egg in the container of a blender. Purée until liquified. Add half of the diced potatoes and purée until smooth, but not liquified. Transfer the mixture to a bowl. Repeat with the remaining onions, egg and potatoes. Combine the 2 batches in a bowl, add the salt and pepper and blot up any excess liquid with paper towels. Fold in the flour. Cook as directed above.

Potato Latkes; Chunky Applesauce

CHUNKY APPLESAUCE

MAKES 4–5 CUPS (32–40 FL OZ/1–1.2 L)

A traditional companion to potato latkes, this applesauce has a bracing tartness. If you wish, add a little more sugar to taste.

8–10 apples, peeled, cored and cut into
   1-inch (2.5-cm) chunks
juice of 2–3 oranges, about 1 cup
   (8 fl oz/250 ml)
½ cup (4 oz/125 g) sugar or to taste
2 teaspoons grated lemon zest
½ teaspoon ground cinnamon

Place the apples and orange juice in a heavy sauté pan. Cook over moderate heat, stirring often, until the apples start to soften, about 10 minutes. Stir in the sugar, lemon zest and cinnamon and cook, uncovered, until tender but still chunky, about 20–25 minutes. Adjust the seasoning and serve warm. Or cool, cover and refrigerate for up to 2 days. Rewarm before serving.

SPICED BRISKET OF BEEF
SERVES 12

A blend of Middle Eastern spices adds an exotic touch to the classic Jewish braised brisket.

1 brisket of beef, about 10 lb (5 kg)
½ cup (4 oz/125 g) sugar
1 teaspoon ground nutmeg
1 teaspoon ground cloves
1 teaspoon ground allspice
2 tablespoons ground pepper
1 teaspoon ground ginger
6 tablespoons (3 fl oz/90 ml) olive oil
    or chicken fat
salt to taste
12 cups (3 lb/1.5 kg) diced onions
2 cups (16 fl oz/500 ml) beef stock or
    as needed
2 cups (16 fl oz/500 ml) tomato purée
    (see glossary)

*P*lace the meat in a large glass or plastic container. Combine the sugar, nutmeg, cloves, allspice, pepper and ginger and sprinkle them over the meat. Cover and refrigerate for 2 days, turning once each day. Lift the meat from the marinade and pat dry.

❧ Heat 3 tablespoons of the oil or fat in a large heavy frying pan or on a griddle. Sprinkle the meat with salt and brown on both sides. Set aside.

❧ In a heavy pot large enough to hold the brisket, heat the remaining 3 tablespoons oil or fat and cook the onions until tender and translucent, about 10 minutes. Place the beef atop the onions and cover the pot. Reduce the heat and simmer the brisket for 2 hours. Add the beef stock if the onions and beef haven't exuded enough juices;

Spiced Brisket of Beef; Carrot Tsimmes

you will need about 3 cups (24 fl oz/750 ml) of liquid. Add the tomato purée and cook until the meat is tender, about 1 hour longer.

❧ Remove the brisket to a carving board and let rest, covered with aluminum foil, for 10 minutes. Cook the pan juices over medium heat to reduce them if they are too thin or lack flavor. Adjust the seasoning. Slice the meat across the grain and serve with the pan juices.

CARROT TSIMMES
SERVES 12

In Yiddish, the term tsimmes *often describes a messy situation. Add sweet potatoes or dried fruit, if you like, to this flavorful mess.*

1 cup (6 oz/185 g) raisins
3 tablespoons vegetable oil or
    chicken fat
2 onions, sliced thin
24 carrots, peeled and cut into ¼-inch
    (6-mm) slices
6 tablespoons (4 oz/125 g) honey
grated zest of 2 lemons
chicken stock or wine
salt and freshly ground pepper to taste

*S*oak the raisins in hot water to cover for 10 minutes; drain, reserving the raisin water to use in the tsimmes.

❧ Heat the oil or fat in a large saucepan. Add the sliced onions and cook until tender, about 5 minutes. Add the carrots, honey, lemon zest, raisin water and enough stock or wine to cover the carrots. Bring to a boil, reduce heat, cover and simmer until the carrots are tender, about 10–15 minutes. You may need to add a bit more liquid from time to time. Add the raisins in the last 5 minutes. Season with salt and pepper.

Foil-wrapped chocolate coins, known as gelt, are a traditional Hanukkah party favor. Usually given to the children as tokens of prosperity and goodwill, you can set the coins out in a small basket or a net bag, or strew them festively around the table.

PECAN TORTE

MAKES ONE 10-INCH (25-CM) TORTE

The torte includes tangerine zest to link it to its accompanying sorbet. At a non-kosher meal, top it with whipped cream.

3 cups (12 oz/375 g) chopped pecans
1½ cups (12 oz/375 g) sugar
10 eggs, separated
½ cup (4 fl oz/125 ml) fresh
   tangerine juice
grated zest of 3 tangerines
½ cup (2 oz/60 g) sifted all-purpose
   (plain) flour
½ teaspoon salt
1 teaspoon ground cinnamon
chopped candied tangerine peel,
   optional

Preheat an oven to 350°F (180°C). Oil and flour a 10-inch (25-cm) tube pan or angel food cake pan and set aside.

❧ Chop the nuts with ½ cup (4 oz/ 125 g) of the sugar in a food processor as finely as possible; do not let it turn to paste. Set aside.

❧ In the bowl of an electric mixer, combine the egg yolks and ½ cup (4 oz/ 125 g) of the remaining sugar, set the bowl over hot water and whisk for a few minutes until warm. Remove from the hot water and beat on high speed with the whisk attachment until the mixture is very thick and pale and a small amount trailed from the whisk forms a ribbon on the surface of the mixture, about 8 minutes. Stir in the tangerine juice and zest.

❧ In a bowl, toss the nut mixture with the flour, salt and cinnamon, then gradually fold these dry ingredients into the yolks with a rubber spatula.

❧ In a large bowl, beat the egg whites until soft peaks form. Gradually beat in the remaining ½ cup (4 oz/125 g) sugar. Fold the whites into the batter. Fold in the optional candied peel. Pour the batter into the prepared pan and bake until a toothpick inserted in the center of the cake comes out clean, about 45 minutes. Let cool in the pan, then invert onto a plate; slice to serve.

TANGERINE SORBET

MAKES ABOUT 4 CUPS (32 FL OZ/1 L)

Whole tangerines, at their peak during the holidays, are traditionally given as gifts to children at the Hanukkah feast. Be sure to grate the zest before juicing the fruit.

4 cups (32 fl oz/1 l) fresh tangerine juice
1½ cups (12 oz/375 g) sugar
1 tablespoon fresh lemon juice
2 tablespoons grated tangerine zest

Combine 2 cups (16 fl oz/500 ml) of the tangerine juice and the sugar in small saucepan. Cook, stirring occasionally, until the sugar dissolves and the mixture is clear. Set aside and let cool. Stir in the remaining tangerine juice and lemon juice. Add the zest. Freeze in an ice cream maker according to the manufacturer's instructions.

Pecan Torte; Tangerine Sorbet

CHRISTMAS SEASON OPEN HOUSE

AT NO OTHER TIME OF YEAR are we more likely to invite friends and family to drop by than during December. Holiday gatherings, whether for traditional gift exchanges or simply to share good cheer, call for a menu that can be prepared in advance and served buffet-style.

Our Christmas season open house takes place in a living room, where guests can comfortably mingle around the tree and beside the hearth. Traditional ornaments play the major role in setting the party's scene. You'll probably want to supplement yours with an abundance of seasonal touches; pine cones, boughs of holly and sprigs of mistletoe, wreaths of various sizes and myriad glowing candles fill the room with warmth and merriment. If you have a fireplace and the weather is cold, keep the flames roaring all day long.

THIS CHRISTMAS BUFFET menu for eighteen is as robust and warming as the season itself. There are light dishes for guests who just want to nibble, as well as hearty recipes for those who want a complete meal.

To arrange separate stations for serving the different dishes, clear coffee tables, side tables and other surfaces in a living room, dining room or den. Present the biscotti, cheese and pâté arranged on platters to welcome newcomers. The pizza, blintzes and duck may be replenished hot from the oven as the afternoon or evening progresses. A variety of other beverages, including a favorite hot cider or cocoa, may be served as well as the wine.

Menu

A punch bowl of cider mulled with citrus zests, sugar and sweet spices offers holiday warmth to guests on arrival.

WINE RECOMMENDATIONS

Offer both white and red. For the white, pour a medium-to-full-bodied assertive wine with notes of spice and earth: a rustic Pinot Blanc or a flinty Chardonnay. For the red, try an Australian Shiraz or a simple French country wine such as Madiran or Corbières. With dessert, offer a Malmsey Madeira or a brown or cream sherry from Spain.

Savory Biscotti

Herbed Cheese Spread

Country Pâté

❧

Potato & Onion Pizza

Mushroom Blintzes

Duck with Lentils

❧

*Chestnut Torte with Chocolate
Mocha Butter Cream*

*An ensemble of natural decorations, including pine
cones, oranges, fir boughs and cranberries, flanks a log
birdhouse to create a miniature winter scene. Finch eggs
fill the tiny bird's nest.*

PREPARATION LIST

◆ Up to 2 weeks ahead, prepare the pâté.

◆ Up to 2 days ahead, make the biscotti and
store them in an airtight container; make and
refrigerate the cheese spread.

◆ The day before, roast and cut up the ducks;
make the lentils. Refrigerate them separately.

◆ The morning of the party, make and refrigerate the crêpes. Make and refrigerate the torte.

◆ Several hours ahead, make the pizza dough
and toppings, to be assembled and baked just
before serving.

THE FOLLOWING MENU SERVES 18 GUESTS;
FOR A SMALLER PARTY, OFFER FEWER DISHES.

*Napkins in a plaid
pattern of traditional
holiday colors are folded
as buffet servers (see
page 183) to hold
knives and forks.*

Everybody loves crunchy fresh vegetables, especially when served along with rich holiday fare. Present spears of cucumbers and carrots, endive leaves, crisp scallions and cherry tomatoes near the biscotti and herbed cheese spread for guests to snack on. Use double old-fashioned glasses or French confiture jars to hold each kind of crudité upright.

SAVORY BISCOTTI

MAKES 48 BISCOTTI

Make a double batch so you'll have extra throughout the holidays. Recrisp them on a baking sheet in a 350°F (180°C) oven for 5 minutes.

1 cup (8 oz/250 g) unsalted butter at room temperature
1 cup (8 oz/250 g) sugar
6 eggs
2 tablespoons aquavit (see glossary)
4½ cups (1⅓ lb/665 g) all-purpose (plain) flour
2 teaspoons salt
1 tablespoon baking powder
¼ cup (2 oz/60 g) toasted cumin seeds, crushed (see glossary)
3 tablespoons toasted caraway seeds, crushed (see glossary)
2 cups (8 oz/250 g) ground toasted walnuts (see glossary)

Preheat an oven to 350°F (180°C). In a large bowl, beat the butter and sugar until fluffy. Add the eggs and aquavit and beat well. Add the flour, salt, baking powder, cumin seeds, caraway seeds and walnuts and mix until blended. Form into 4 oval logs and place on 2 ungreased baking sheets. Bake until golden brown and firm to the touch, about 30 minutes. Remove from the oven and let cool on a rack for about 10 minutes.

⁓ Reduce the oven temperature to 250°F (120°C). Cut the logs diagonally into ½-inch (12-mm) slices and lay the slices flat on the baking sheets. Bake until dried, about 8–10 minutes longer. Let cool, then store in an airtight container for up to 2 days, or freeze for longer storage.

HERBED CHEESE SPREAD

MAKES ABOUT 5 CUPS (40 OZ/1.25 KG)

Influenced by Italian, French and Romanian dishes, this creamy spread is also good on pumpernickel bread with watercress and cucumber. It can be made up to 2 days in advance.

3 tablespoons olive oil or unsalted butter
1 tablespoon minced garlic
3 cups (15 oz/470 g) crumbled mild fresh goat cheese or feta cheese
1–2 cups (8–16 oz/250–500 g) ricotta
¼ cup (⅜ oz/10 g) chopped fresh parsley
¼ cup (⅜ oz/10 g) minced fresh chives
2 tablespoons finely chopped fresh thyme
2 teaspoons freshly ground pepper

In a small frying pan, heat the oil or melt the butter over moderate heat, add the garlic and cook until tender but not colored, about 3 minutes. Transfer to a food processor or blender and add the goat or feta cheese, 1 cup of the ricotta, the parsley, chives, thyme and pepper. Process to combine. Taste and add more ricotta if goat cheese flavor is too strong. Transfer to a small crock or serving dish. Cover and refrigerate until serving time.

Savory Biscotti; Herbed Cheese Spread

COUNTRY PÂTÉ

MAKES THREE 9- BY 5- BY 3-INCH
(23- BY 13- BY 7.5-CM) PÂTÉS

Weighting is essential to compact these pâtés. Use another loaf pan or a flat object that fits inside the rim, topped with kitchen weights, heavy cans or bricks. Children's building blocks work in a pinch, too.

1 lb (500 g) finely ground veal
2 lb (1 kg) finely ground pork shoulder
½ lb (250 g) pork fat, coarsely ground
2 lb (1 kg) chicken livers
¼ cup (2 fl oz/60 ml) heavy
   (double) cream
½ cup (3 oz/90 g) all-purpose
   (plain) flour
3 eggs
½ cup (4 fl oz/125 ml) Cognac
   or Armagnac
8 large cloves garlic
1 teaspoon ground nutmeg
½ teaspoon ground allspice
½ teaspoon ground ginger
½ teaspoon ground cinnamon

4 teaspoons salt
2 teaspoons freshly ground pepper
9–12 bay leaves
6 thin sheets pork fat (2 combined should
   be large enough to cover each loaf)
3 large baguettes, sliced
cornichon pickles

℘reheat an oven to 400°F (200°C). Oil three 9- by 5- by 3-inch (23- by 13- by 7.5-cm) loaf pans and set aside. Combine the ground veal, ground pork and fat in a large bowl. Combine the livers, cream, flour, eggs, Cognac or Armagnac, garlic, nutmeg, allspice, ginger, cinnamon, salt and pepper in a large food processor (or in a blender, in batches) and purée. Combine with the ground meat and mix until well blended.

℘ Pour the mixture into the prepared loaf pans. Top each loaf with a few bay leaves and 2 sheets of fat cut to fit the pan. Cover the loaf pans with a double thickness of aluminum foil. Place the loaf pans in a large baking pan and add hot water to come halfway up the sides.

Country Pâté

℘ Bake for 2 hours. Remove and reserve the aluminum foil. Continue baking until lightly browned, about 20 minutes longer. Remove from the oven and re-cover with the foil. Place another loaf pan on top of each pâté and weight it with heavy tins. Let the pâtés sit until cool. Chill well. These pâtés will keep for about 2 weeks under refrigeration. To serve, unmold the pâtés, slice and offer with baguettes and cornichons.

POTATO & ONION PIZZA

SERVES 18

Instead of mixing prosciutto strips with the onions, thin slices of the ham may be draped over the pizza after baking.

FOR THE CRUST:
1 tablespoon active dry yeast
1¼ cups (10 fl oz/300 ml) warm
   (110°F/43°C) water
3½ cups (1⅛ lb/560 g) unbleached
   all-purpose (plain) flour
⅓ cup (1½ oz/45 g) rye or buckwheat
   flour or an additional ⅓ cup
   (2 oz/60 g) all-purpose (plain) flour
3 tablespoons olive oil
1 teaspoon salt
3 tablespoons finely chopped
   fresh rosemary

FOR THE TOPPING:
8 small red new potatoes
6 tablespoons (3 fl oz/90 ml) olive oil
salt and freshly ground pepper to taste
4 large onions, sliced thin
1 cup (4 oz/125 g) long, thin prosciutto
   strips, optional
cornmeal for sprinkling
1 tablespoon minced garlic
1–1½ cups (4–6 oz/125–185 g)
   grated mozzarella
2 tablespoons chopped fresh sage
   or rosemary
½ cup (2 oz/60 g) freshly grated Parmesan

Potato & Onion Pizza

To make the crust, dissolve the yeast in ½ cup (4 fl oz/125 ml) of the warm water in the bowl of an electric mixer. Add ½ cup (2½ oz/75 g) of the all-purpose (plain) flour and mix to combine. Cover and let sit for about 30 minutes.

❧ Add the remaining all-purpose flour, buckwheat flour, remaining water, olive oil, salt and rosemary and mix well. Beat on low speed with the dough hook attached until the dough leaves the sides of the bowl cleanly, about 10 minutes. Or, to make by hand, knead on a lightly floured board for about 10 minutes, or until the dough is no longer sticky. Transfer the dough to an oiled bowl, cover with a towel and let rise in a warm place until doubled, about 1 hour.

❧ Meanwhile, to make the topping, preheat an oven to 400°F (200°C). Place the potatoes in a small baking pan. Brush the potatoes with 1 tablespoon of the olive oil, sprinkle with salt and pepper and roast for 25–30 minutes, or until cooked through but firm. Let cool, then cut into ¼-inch-thick (6-mm) slices.

❧ Heat 3 more tablespoons of the oil in a large sauté pan, add the onions and cook, stirring occasionally, until tender and translucent, about 10 minutes. Caramelize the onions by continuing to cook them until golden, if desired. Season with salt and pepper and stir in the prosciutto, if using. Set aside.

❧ Turn the dough out onto a lightly floured board. Shape into a ball. Cover and allow to rest in the refrigerator for 30 minutes. Meanwhile, preheat an oven to 475°F (240°C).

❧ Roll and stretch the dough into 1 large rectangle; place on a baking sheet sprinkled with cornmeal. Mix the garlic and the remaining 2 tablespoons oil and spread over the dough. Top with the mozzarella, then with the cooked onions and potatoes. Sprinkle with the chopped sage or rosemary and the Parmesan. Bake until the edges are golden brown and puffed, about 12–15 minutes. Brush the edges of the pizza with additional olive oil to add a shine, if desired.

MUSHROOM BLINTZES
MAKES 36 BLINTZES

In this Russian-inspired dish, thin crêpes, or blini, are folded around a mushroom filling in neat parcels resembling Jewish deli blintzes.

FOR THE CRÊPES:
1 cup (8 fl oz/250 ml) cold water
1 cup (8 fl oz/250 ml) cold milk
4 eggs
½ teaspoon salt
2 cups (8 oz/250 g) sifted all-purpose
 (plain) flour
¼ cup (2 oz/60 g) unsalted butter, melted

FOR THE FILLING:
8 tablespoons (4 oz/125 g) unsalted
 butter, plus additional for cooking
 blintzes
2 cups (10 oz/315 g) finely chopped
 onions
1½ lb (750 g) fresh mushrooms,
 chopped coarsely
2 teaspoons minced garlic
4 teaspoons chopped fresh thyme or
 5 tablespoons (½ oz/15 g) chopped
 fresh dill
3–4 tablespoons all-purpose (plain) flour
⅓ cup (3 fl oz/90 ml) Madeira
 or sherry
½ cup (4 fl oz/125 ml) chicken stock,
 if needed
salt and freshly ground pepper to taste

TO COOK AND SERVE THE BLINTZES:
12 tablespoons (6 oz/180 g) unsalted
 butter
sour cream, optional

To make the crêpes, put the water, milk, eggs and salt in a blender or food processor. Add the flour and melted butter and blend until smooth. Cover and let the batter rest in the refrigerator for about 2 hours.

Lightly butter a small (about 7-in/18-cm) crêpe pan or small nonstick sauté pan and place it over moderate heat. Ladle 2 tablespoons of batter into the pan and swirl it around until it coats the bottom of the pan. Let cook for a minute or two until set and not shiny. Loosen the crêpe with a spatula, then flip it or turn it with both hands and cook for 30 seconds on the other side. Slide the crêpe out of the pan. Repeat until all the batter is used, stacking the cooked crêpes.

To make the filling, melt 3 tablespoons of the butter in a sauté pan over moderate heat and cook the onions until tender and translucent, about 10 minutes. Lift out and set aside. Melt the remaining 5 tablespoons (2½ oz/80 g) butter in the pan as needed and cook the mushrooms in batches over very high heat so they don't give off too much liquid, about 5 minutes. Place all the cooked mushrooms in the pan and add the garlic. Cook for 1 minute, return the onions to the pan, add the thyme or dill and flour and cook for 3 minutes, stirring constantly. Add the Madeira or sherry and cook until the mixture holds together, 3–4 minutes; if too dry, add enough stock to moisten. Season with salt and pepper.

To assemble the blintzes, place 2 generous tablespoons of filling in the center of each crêpe. Tuck in the sides and fold the top over the bottom edge to make a neat packet. Repeat until all the filling is used. Melt about 2 tablespoons of the butter in a sauté pan and fry the blintzes in batches of 6 until golden on both sides. Keep warm, covered with aluminum foil. Repeat, adding the remaining butter as needed, until all the blintzes are cooked. Serve with dollops of sour cream, if desired.

DUCK WITH LENTILS
SERVES 18

Based on traditional French and Italian winter fare, this recipe extracts more fat from the ducks by roasting instead of braising them. If you have only one small oven, roast the ducks two at a time.

FOR THE DUCKS:
6 ducks, about 5 lb (2.5 kg) each, necks
 and wing tips removed and reserved,
 and excess fat removed
12 cloves garlic, minced
grated zest of 6 large lemons
2 tablespoons salt
2 tablespoons freshly ground pepper
12 fresh thyme or marjoram sprigs
3 lemons, cut into quarters

FOR THE LENTILS:
6 cups (2½ lb/1.25 kg) lentils,
 preferably French green lentils
14 cups (3½ qt/3.5 l) water
½ cup (4 oz/125 g) unsalted butter
6 large onions, diced, about 6 cups
 (1½ lb/750 g)
6 large carrots, peeled and cut into
 ¼-inch (6-mm) dice
3 ribs celery, cut into ¼-inch
 (6-mm) dice
2 tablespoons minced garlic
1 teaspoon ground cinnamon
2 teaspoons ground cumin
4 Pippin or other tart green apples,
 peeled, cored and diced
2 cups (16 fl oz/500 ml) chicken stock
½ cup (¾ oz/20 g) chopped fresh
 parsley
3 tablespoons chopped fresh thyme
 or marjoram
2 tablespoons grated lemon zest
salt and freshly ground pepper to taste

To prepare the ducks, preheat an oven or ovens to 475°F (240°C). Place 2 ducks on a rack in each of 3 large roasting pans. Prick the ducks evenly all over with a fork. Mash together the garlic, lemon zest, salt and pepper and spread this over the inside and outside of the birds. Place the herbs and lemon quarters inside the ducks. Roast until they are tender and well browned and the juices run clear when the thighs are pierced with a knife, about 1 hour. Let sit until cool enough to handle, then cut the ducks into quarters with shears, cutting off and discarding the backbones. Set aside.

Meanwhile, to make the lentils, combine them with the water in a large pot and bring to a boil. Reduce the heat and simmer, covered, until the lentils are tender but still firm to the bite, about 20 minutes for brown lentils, or up to 25–40 minutes for green lentils. Test them every 5–10 minutes for doneness. Remove from the heat and set aside.

Melt the butter in a large sauté pan with high sides and cook the onions, carrots and celery over moderate heat, stirring occasionally, until they are tender, about 15 minutes. Add the garlic, cinnamon, cumin and apples and cook for 1–2 minutes. Add the lentils and their cooking liquid, stock, herbs and lemon zest; cover and simmer until all the flavors are blended, about 5 minutes. Season to taste with salt and pepper and adjust the spices to taste. The duck and the lentils can be cooked to this point up to 1 day ahead and refrigerated separately.

To serve, combine the duck pieces and lentils in a large heatproof casserole, cover with aluminum foil and place in a preheated 400°F (200°C) oven until bubbly and hot, about 25 minutes.

Mushroom Blintzes; Duck with Lentils

Chestnut Torte with Chocolate Mocha Butter Cream

SERVES 12

Chestnuts, synonymous with winter holidays, combine with a chocolate mocha butter cream for an intensely rich dessert. Look for glacéed chestnuts in specialty food shops or an Italian market.

FOR THE TORTE:
6 large eggs, separated
1½ cups (12 oz/375 g) sugar
1 tablespoon vanilla extract (essence)
2 cups (1 lb/500 g) chestnut purée, pushed through a sieve
1 cup (4 oz/125 g) almonds, finely ground

FOR THE CHOCOLATE MOCHA BUTTER CREAM:
8 oz (250 g) bittersweet chocolate
¼ cup (2 fl oz/60 ml) strong coffee
4 egg yolks
1 cup (8 oz/250 g) sugar
⅓ cup (3 fl oz/90 ml) water
1½ cups (12 oz/375 g) unsalted butter, cut into pieces
3 tablespoons dark rum

FOR THE GARNISH:
whole glacéed chestnuts

Preheat an oven to 350°F (180°C). Butter and flour two 8-inch (20-cm) springform pans.

❧ To prepare the torte, place the egg yolks and 1 cup (8 oz/250 g) of the sugar in the bowl of an electric mixer, set the bowl over hot water and whisk for a few minutes until warm. Remove from the hot water and beat on high speed with the whisk attachment until the mixture is very thick and pale and a small amount trailed from the whisk forms a ribbon on the surface of the mixture, about 8 minutes. Beat in the vanilla, then fold in the chestnut purée and the ground almonds.

❧ Beat the egg whites until soft peaks form, then gradually beat in the remaining ½ cup (4 oz/125 g) sugar until the mixture is stiff but not dry. Stir one third of the whites into the chestnut mixture, then fold in the rest. Divide the batter between the 2 prepared pans and bake until the cakes are pale gold and pull away from the sides of the pans, about 40–50 minutes. Let cool in the pans on racks. Loosen the edges with a knife and then remove the pan sides.

❧ To make the butter cream, combine the chocolate and coffee in the top of a double boiler and melt over simmering water. Set aside and keep warm. Place the egg yolks in the bowl of an electric mixer, set the bowl over hot water and whisk for a few minutes until warm. Remove from the hot water and beat on high speed with the whisk attachment until thick and pale.

❧ Meanwhile, combine the sugar and water in a small saucepan and bring to a boil over high heat, stirring until the sugar dissolves. Boil rapidly until the sugar reaches 236°F (113°C) on a candy thermometer. With the mixer on low speed, gradually beat the hot syrup into the beaten yolks. Fold in the chocolate mixture. Beat in the butter a little at a time. Add the dark rum. Chill until thick enough to spread.

❧ To assemble, place 1 cake on a serving plate, frost it, then place the second cake on top. Frost the top and sides. Refrigerate until the frosting is set, then bring to room temperature for serving. Top with glacéed chestnuts.

Chestnut Torte with Chocolate Mocha Butter Cream

$\mathcal{H}$ERITAGE CHRISTMAS DINNER

MOST OF US LAVISH MORE attention on the Yuletide dinner than on any other meal of the year. Whether celebrated on Christmas Eve or Christmas Day, or both, the occasion brings back memories of holidays past and we usually turn faithfully to family traditions when planning the meal.

We set our Christmas dinner in a formal dining room alongside a roaring fire. Rather than conceal the table's beautiful wood surface, we placed an ornate fabric runner down its center; an extra-wide ribbon would work as well. We decked the mantel and table with wreaths, bouquets of pine and lilies, silver bowls filled with cranberries and strands of colored beads. Our Christmas tree centerpiece is a variation on the easy-to-make Holiday Tree (see page 185). You could make a large one for the main table and smaller ones to go alongside, as shown on these pages.

China accented in gold gleams at a holiday place setting decorated with fresh cranberries and golden beads.

F OR CHRISTMAS MENU INSPIRATION, we looked to the Old World, including dishes that have been handed down to us through the generations. The recipes that follow reflect a diversity of European cuisines, with an appetizer and dessert from France, an Italian-inspired salad and side dishes and a traditional English roast beef.

During this busy time of year, careful organization is essential to enjoying the holidays. It's a good idea to begin planning Christmas dinner at least several weeks in advance by reading through the preparation list and recipes. To ensure that you get the best prime or choice beef roast, order it well ahead of time from a quality butcher shop.

Menu

Achieve lavish results with little effort by attaching gold ornaments to calla lilies and holiday greens.

Onion Tart

Radicchio, Fennel & Walnut Salad

❧

*Rib-Eye Roast
with Mustard & Black Pepper*

*Winter Greens
with Pancetta & Mint*

Potato & Sage Gratin

❧

*Apple Charlotte
with Brandied Whipped Cream
& Apricot Sauce*

PREPARATION LIST

◆ The day before, make the tart crust.

◆ The morning of the dinner, make the charlotte, to be rewarmed and unmolded before serving.

◆ Up to 3 hours before dinner, coat the roast with its seasoning spread; prepare the salad ingredients and the dressing.

◆ Up to 2 hours ahead, assemble the gratin.

◆ Just before serving, cook the winter greens and toss the salad.

EACH RECIPE YIELDS 6 SERVINGS.

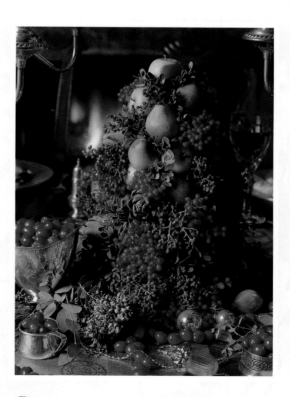

Baby pears, lady apples, artichokes and seasonal berries and greens are affixed to an artificial base for this variation on the Holiday Tree (page 185).

WINE RECOMMENDATIONS

Begin with a white from the Pacific Northwest, such as an Oregon Pinot Gris or, if you prefer red wine, a Pinot Noir. With the beef, pour an elegant, full-bodied Bordeaux, or an aged Rhône such as Châteauneuf-du-Pape. After dessert, pass quality Calvados or Cognac.

The facets of a cut-glass decanter highlight the deep color and clarity of fine red wine poured to accompany the Christmas dinner.

ONION TART

MAKES ONE 9-INCH (23-CM) TART

Serve slices of this classic French quiche as a first course with the radicchio and fennel salad.

basic pie pastry for a single-crust pie
  shell (recipe on page 177)
1½ lb (750 g) large onions
¼ cup (2 oz/60 g) unsalted butter
2 tablespoons oil
salt, freshly ground pepper and ground
  nutmeg to taste
4 eggs
1½ cups (12 fl oz/375 ml) heavy
  (double) cream

*R*oll out the pastry dough and use it to line a 9-inch (23-cm) pie pan. Flute the edges and set the shell aside in the freezer for 30 minutes or overnight.
❧ Peel the onions, cut them into quarters and slice thin. Heat the butter and oil in a large sauté pan over moderate-low heat. Add the onions and cook, stirring occasionally, until they are golden brown and starting to caramelize, about 30 minutes. Season the onions with salt, pepper and nutmeg.
❧ Preheat an oven to 375°F (190°C). Place the onions in the bottom of the pie shell. In a bowl, beat together the eggs and cream and season with salt and pepper. Pour the mixture over the onions and bake the tart on the middle rack of the oven until set and golden, 30–40 minutes. Let sit for 10 minutes, then slice and serve.

RADICCHIO, FENNEL & WALNUT SALAD

SERVES 6

Italian in style, this pretty salad combines mildly bitter and sweet tastes that nicely counterpoint the onion tart.

3 heads radicchio
3 small fennel bulbs
6 tablespoons (3 fl oz/90 ml) toasted
  walnut oil
2 tablespoons olive oil
3–4 tablespoons balsamic vinegar
salt and freshly ground pepper to taste
1 cup (4 oz/125 g) toasted walnuts
  (see glossary)

*T*rim the ends from the radicchio and separate the leaves. Wash well if sandy and dry well. Remove the tubular stems from the fennel and cut the bulbs into quarters; remove the hard center cores and any discolored outer portions. Slice thin.
❧ In a bowl, combine the walnut oil, olive oil and vinegar to taste with a whisk. Season to taste with salt and pepper. Marinate the walnuts in ¼ cup (2 fl oz/60 ml) of the vinaigrette for 15 minutes. Toss the radicchio, fennel and walnuts in the remaining vinaigrette. Divide among 6 salad plates.

Onion Tart; Radicchio, Fennel & Walnut Salad

RIB-EYE ROAST WITH MUSTARD & BLACK PEPPER

SERVES 6

To ensure perfectly cooked beef, use an instant-read meat thermometer. You should have plenty left over for sandwiches.

FOR THE ROAST:
4–5 lb (2–2.5 kg) rib-eye roast
4 cloves garlic, cut into slivers
1 cup (8 oz/250 g) Dijon mustard
¼ cup (2 fl oz/60 ml) soy sauce
4 tablespoons (2 oz/60 g) coarsely
   ground or cracked pepper

FOR THE SAUCE:
¼ cup (2 oz/60 g) Dijon mustard
1 tablespoon soy sauce
1 cup (8 fl oz/250 ml) beef stock
1 tablespoon cracked pepper

To prepare the roast, cut incisions at even intervals in the surface of the meat and insert slivers of garlic. Place the meat in a roasting pan. Combine the mustard and soy sauce and spread the mixture over the roast. Top with the pepper. Let the roast sit at room temperature for up to 3 hours.

Preheat an oven to 350°F (180°C). Roast the meat until a meat thermometer inserted in the center of the roast reads 120°F (50°C) for rare, about 1½ hours. Remove from the oven and let rest on a carving board, covered with aluminum foil, for 15 minutes.

To make the sauce, in a small pan combine the mustard, soy sauce, beef stock and pepper with a whisk and heat through. Or, pour the stock into the degreased drippings in the roasting pan and stir to free any browned bits. Whisk in the mustard, soy sauce and pepper.

WINTER GREENS WITH PANCETTA & MINT

SERVES 6

Mint and pancetta perfectly offset the mild bitterness of the greens. Make this at the absolute last moment for the freshest color and taste.

¼ cup (2 fl oz/60 ml) olive oil
8 slices bacon or pancetta, about
   ¼ inch (6 mm) thick, cut into dice
   or small strips
1 large onion, chopped, about 2 cups
   (8 oz/250 g)
3 cloves garlic, minced
¼ cup (2 fl oz/60 ml) red wine
   vinegar
1½ lb (750 g) well-washed greens
   (dandelion, kale, chard, mustard
   greens or a combination), stemmed
   and cut into thin strips
salt and freshly ground pepper to taste
6 tablespoons chopped fresh mint

Heat the olive oil in a large sauté pan with high sides. Add the diced bacon or pancetta and cook until translucent but not browned, about 3 minutes. Add the onion and cook until soft, about 8 minutes. Add the garlic and cook for 1–2 minutes. Add the vinegar and greens and cover the pan. Cook the greens until wilted, stirring occasionally, about 5 minutes. Season with salt and pepper and stir in the fresh mint just before serving.

POTATO & SAGE GRATIN

SERVES 6

Fresh sage leaves and a hint of nutmeg perfume this classic dish of sliced and baked potatoes.

3 cups (24 fl oz/750 ml) heavy
   (double) cream
4 cloves garlic, sliced
8–10 fresh sage leaves, chopped, plus
   whole sage leaves for garnish
1½ teaspoons salt
1 teaspoon freshly ground pepper
¼ teaspoon ground nutmeg
6 large white boiling potatoes

Preheat an oven to 375°F (190°C). Butter a 12-cup (3-qt/3-l) baking dish. In a saucepan, bring the cream to a boil with the garlic and sage. Lower the heat and simmer for 15 minutes. Season with salt, pepper and nutmeg.

Peel and slice the potatoes ¼ inch (6 mm) thick. Layer the potatoes in overlapping rows in the baking dish and pour the cream with sage and garlic over them. The cream should just cover the potatoes; if not, add a bit more. Cover with aluminum foil and set aside for up to 2 hours. Bake for 30 minutes, then remove the foil and continue to bake until potatoes are tender but still hold their shape, about 20 minutes longer. Garnish with a few whole sage leaves to serve.

Rib-Eye Roast with Mustard & Black Pepper;
Potato & Sage Gratin; Winter Greens with Pancetta & Mint

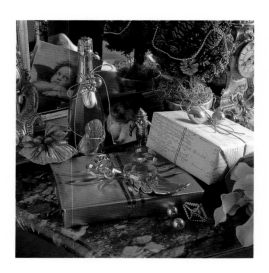

Gold tones set the theme for a beguiling display of presents. Yet these elegant touches need not be costly. Use widely available Christmas ribbon, beads and ornaments in amber hues. To make pine cones gleam like treasures, spray them lightly with gold paint. Tuck a favorite card in a gilded mirror or picture frame.

APPLE CHARLOTTE WITH BRANDIED WHIPPED CREAM & APRICOT SAUCE

SERVES 6

For the most festive presentation, prepare the charlotte in a large mold. The apple purée must be very thick to support the bread casing, so cook it until you get the right consistency.

FOR THE CHARLOTTE:
12 Macintosh, Empire or Rome Beauty
    apples, peeled, cored and cubed
12 tablespoons (6 oz/180 g) unsalted
    butter, melted
¾ cup (6 oz/185 g) granulated sugar
½ teaspoon ground cinnamon
1 tablespoon grated lemon zest
1 teaspoon vanilla extract (essence)
12–15 slices white bread, about ¼
    inch (6 mm) thick, crusts removed

FOR THE BRANDIED WHIPPED CREAM:
1 cup (8 fl oz/250 ml) heavy
    (double) cream
¼ cup (1½ oz/45 g) sifted
    confectioners' (icing) sugar
3 tablespoons brandy, optional

FOR THE APRICOT SAUCE:
1 cup (8 oz/250 g) apricot jam
¼ cup (2 fl oz/60 ml) water
¼ cup (2 fl oz/60 ml) brandy, optional

FOR THE GARNISH:
apricot halves, optional
orange peel, optional

Preheat an oven to 425°F (220°C). In a large, heavy sauté pan over moderate heat, cook the apples with 2 tablespoons of the butter for about 5 minutes. Add the sugar, cinnamon and lemon zest and combine well. Cook until the apples break down into a very thick purée, about 15 minutes. Stir in the vanilla. If the apples are very tart, add a bit more sugar. You should have about 5–6 cups (40–48 fl oz/1.2–1.5 l) apple purée.

❧ Cut the bread into pieces to fit the bottom and sides of a 6-cup (48–fl oz/1.5-l) round charlotte mold or soufflé dish. Dip the bread in the remaining melted butter and place, without overlapping, on the bottom and sides of the mold or dish. Spoon in the apple mixture and top with the remaining bread.

❧ Bake on the lower rack of the oven for 10 minutes, then reduce the oven temperature to 350°F (180°C) and bake until the bread is golden, about 30 minutes longer. Let the charlotte sit for 30 minutes before unmolding. (Or let sit for several hours, then rewarm in a low oven, then unmold.)

❧ To make the brandied whipped cream, in a bowl beat the cream and sugar until it forms soft peaks. Fold in the brandy, if desired. To make the apricot sauce, stir together the jam and water in a small saucepan and warm over low heat. Stir in the brandy if desired. Top the charlotte with some of the whipped cream and serve with the remaining whipped cream and the apricot sauce. Garnish with the apricot halves and orange peel, if desired.

Apple Charlotte with Brandied Whipped Cream & Apricot Sauce

NEW YEAR'S EVE FOR SIX

WITH THE NEW YEAR COMES A SPIRIT of optimism and an eager anticipation of new achievements, of resolutions soon to be fulfilled. As a result, New Year's Eve celebrations can be the most sparkling events of the year. This is a good time to invite your closest friends for a celebratory evening that doesn't end until well after midnight.

To observe New Year's Eve in style, we planned a sit-down dinner for six, to be served late in the evening. We selected elegant floral arrangements, including white tulips, roses, narcissus and orchids with green hydrangeas and bay laurel, but you can use any kind of blossoms, greens, or potted plants to make the setting as informal or formal as you wish. A party favor, wrapped in silver foil and streamers, adds intrigue to each place setting.

To highlight the once-a-year mood of New Year's, we chose to splurge with a menu featuring duck livers, lobster, shrimp, scallops and crème brulée, the richest of custards. The star of the meal is a hands-on bouillabaisse, the classic Provençal fish soup. For this course, you might want to provide your guests with oversized bib napkins to use.

To help you put together this special meal, consult the preparation list at right and the tips given with each recipe. The soup can be prepared in steps so that the last minute cooking is minimal. You could also serve fewer dishes or incorporate recipes from other menus in this book, if you like. The most important thing is to plan the evening so that you can enjoy the revelries as much as your guests.

Menu

A richly polished dining table reflects the elegance of fine silver, china, crystal and white floral arrangements.

WINE RECOMMENDATIONS

Start with a non-vintage brut Champagne, or a sparkling wine from California or Spain. Then move on to either a Chardonnay-based cuvée Champagne, or, if you want a still wine, a bracing white such as French Muscadet or Chablis. With dessert and midnight toasting, pour an extra-dry or demi-sec sparkling wine or Champagne.

*Duck Livers
with Apple-Ginger Butter*

Rice Croquettes

❧

Winter Bouillabaisse

Green Salad

❧

Blood Orange Crème Brulée

Ginger Florentines

*A side table holds a silver coffee service. Beside it,
leather-bound books form a casually elegant backdrop.*

PREPARATION LIST

◆ The day before, prepare the apple-ginger
butter; assemble the croquettes; make the florentines and store them in an airtight container.

◆ The morning of the party, make the soup
base, prepare and refrigerate the aïoli and the
rouille and clean the seafood for the bouillabaisse. Make the crème brulée custard.

◆ One hour before, prepare the potatoes,
fennel and bread for the soup.

◆ Fifteen minutes before guests arrive, cook
the livers and croquettes. Bring the soup base
to a simmer. Just before serving, finish the
soup and the crème brulée.

EACH RECIPE YIELDS 6 SERVINGS.

Silver mint julep cups serve as vases for roses and narcissus.

DUCK LIVERS WITH APPLE-GINGER BUTTER

SERVES 6

Perfumed by the apples and ginger, the duck livers make an unforgettable hors d'oeuvre for a special occasion.

about 6 tablespoons (3 oz/90 g)
 unsalted butter
1 small apple, peeled, cored and finely
 chopped
one 2-inch (5-cm) piece fresh ginger,
 peeled and grated
2 tablespoons Calvados (apple-
 flavored brandy)
salt and freshly ground pepper to taste
12 large duck or chicken livers

In a small sauté pan, melt 2 table-spoons of the butter. Add the apple and ginger and cook until the apple is very soft, about 10–15 minutes. Add the Calvados and cook 1–2 minutes longer. Transfer the mixture to a blender or food processor and purée. Add about 4 tablespoons (2 oz/60 g) of the remaining butter or enough to make a thick, creamy compound. Season with salt and pepper. This butter may be made up to 1 day ahead of time, covered and refrigerated, then softened at room temperature before serving.

Trim the livers carefully of fat and sinew; thread on skewers and sprinkle with salt and pepper. Preheat a broiler (griller). Broil the livers, turning once, until browned on the outside and medium rare in the center, about 2 minutes on each side. Remove the livers from the skewers, place 2 on each plate and top equally with the apple-ginger butter.

RICE CROQUETTES

MAKES 12–16 CROQUETTES

In Italy, these croquettes are known as supplì al telefono, or "telephone wires," which aptly describes the strings formed by biting into their cheese filling.

2 cups (16 fl oz/500 ml) lightly
 salted water
1 cup (7 oz/220 g) Arborio rice
2 eggs, beaten
5 tablespoons (1¼ oz/35 g) freshly
 grated Parmesan cheese
salt, freshly ground pepper and ground
 nutmeg to taste
8 ounces (250 g) fresh mozzarella
 cheese, cut into 12–16 small cubes
1 tablespoon chopped fresh marjoram
 or sage
¾ cup (3 oz/90 g) dried bread crumbs
peanut oil for deep-frying

In a saucepan, bring the water to a boil and stir in the rice; reduce heat and simmer, covered, until it has absorbed all the water and is cooked through but still sticky, about 20 minutes. Stir in the eggs and Parmesan and season with salt, pepper and nutmeg. Spread out evenly in an oiled baking sheet with sides and cool in the refrigerator.

Line a baking sheet with baking parchment and set aside. Roll the cheese cubes in the chopped herb. Scoop up a heaping tablespoonful of the rice, make a well in it and tuck a piece of mozzarella in the center. Push the rice over the cheese and form it into a ball about 1½ inches (4 cm) in diameter. Repeat until all the rice is used. Dip the croquettes in the bread crumbs, place on the lined baking sheet and refrigerate until just before serving (up to 1 day).

To serve, heat about 3 inches (7.5 cm) of peanut oil in a deep-fat fryer or wok to 350°F (180°C). Drop in a few croquettes at a time and fry until golden brown, lifting them in and out of the oil a few times with a slotted spoon so that the cheese will have time to melt in the center before the croquettes get too brown. Drain on paper towels and keep warm in a low oven for no more than 10 minutes before serving. Repeat until all the croquettes are cooked; serve at once.

New Year's Eve is synonymous with effervescence, so position iced champagne and several crystal flutes near the entryway, then pour a welcoming glassful for each guest as he or she arrives.

Rice Croquettes; Duck Livers with Apple-Ginger Butter

NEW YEAR'S BUFFET

THE FIRST DAY OF THE NEW YEAR calls for entertaining of the most relaxed kind. With that in mind, we planned a late-lunch party of familiar, easy-to-eat foods that could be enjoyed while watching televised parades or sports. Whether served midday or in early evening, it's easiest to set the dishes on a coffee table near the fire or the television and let guests serve themselves. To promote a cozier feeling, we pulled in sofas and chairs from around the room.

In keeping with the casual feel of this menu, everyday dishware, cutlery and napkins are the best choice; stack them close by the food. There's no need to fuss over decorations, either. We used a few palm fronds and banana leaves to bring a touch of tropical warmth to the room and incorporated them into the personal artifacts already on display.

165

A serene study in Asian artifacts is an oasis of calm.

Menu

THE FOLLOWING BUFFET MENU is particularly appeal-ing for holiday entertaining because most of it can be made ahead of time and finished just before the guests arrive. These dishes are so versatile, you also could serve them for a New Year's Eve party, an après-ski gathering or a Sunday supper. In fact, any chilly day of the year would be appropriate for this medley of soup, salad and sandwiches.

You could begin the meal with bowls of black bean soup set atop dinner plates; place the quesadillas along-side. These plates can then be used for the sandwiches, potatoes and salad, while dessert can be eaten out of hand. The plan for this party is to make life easy for both the guests and the host, a great way to start the year.

A wooden planter, left on the deck or moved inside, becomes an ice chest for beer and mineral water.

Quesadillas

Black Bean Soup
with Dark Rum & Orange Zest

❧

Barbecued Chicken Sandwiches

Sweet & White Potato Gratin

Spinach Salad with Pecans
& Balsamic Vinaigrette

❧

Chocolate Pound Cake

PREPARATION LIST

◆ Up to 1 month ahead, make and refrigerate the barbecue sauce.

◆ The day before, make the soup and bake the pound cake.

◆ The morning of the party, wash and stem the spinach and prepare the dressing; assemble the quesadillas, to be fried before serving.

◆ Up to several hours before, assemble and bake the potato gratin, to be rewarmed before serving.

EACH RECIPE YIELDS 12 SERVINGS.

WINE RECOMMENDATIONS

To complement the somewhat spicy food, select a slightly smoky red wine loaded with ripe fruit, such as Zinfandel or Burgundy. If you wish to continue toasting the new year, pour a rose Champagne or sparkling wine. Beer could also be enjoyed throughout the meal; choose a medium-bodied amber ale or lager. For dessert, add a dash of Kahlúa to the coffee.

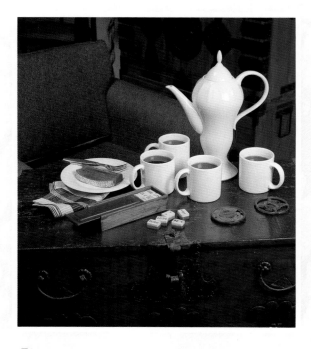

Set out some classic games, along with mugs of coffee, to amuse guests all afternoon long.

QUESADILLAS

SERVES 12

One of the great snacks of Mexico, these filled tortillas are the Latin American equivalent of the grilled cheese sandwich.

6 large fresh poblano chili peppers
6 ripe avocados
6 cups (1½ lb/750 g) grated Monterey jack cheese
24 flour tortillas
2 cups (6 oz/185 g) finely chopped green (spring) onions
½ cup (¾ oz/20 g) finely chopped cilantro (fresh coriander)
salt and freshly ground pepper to taste
salsa, optional

*R*oast, peel and derib the peppers as directed on page 189. Cut the flesh into ¼-inch (6-mm) dice.

❧ Cut the avocados in half, remove the pit, scoop from the shell with a large spoon and cut into thin slices.

❧ Spread about ¼ cup (1 oz/30 g) grated cheese over half of each tortilla. Top equally with some diced peppers, a few slices of avocado, the minced green onions and cilantro; sprinkle with salt and pepper. Fold each tortilla gently in half without pressing down on it or it will crack. Repeat until all the ingredients are used. Cover and refrigerate until ready to cook (up to several hours).

❧ Place a griddle or large frying pan over medium-high heat and lightly oil it. Place as many filled tortillas as can fit on the griddle or in the pan, weight slightly with a pan lid and cook until golden brown on each side, turning once. Repeat until all the quesadillas are cooked. If desired, cut each quesadilla in half and serve with salsa.

BLACK BEAN SOUP WITH DARK RUM & ORANGE ZEST

SERVES 12

Robust and warming, this Caribbean-style soup gains an unusual twist from rum and citrus.

6 cups (2½ lb/1.25 kg) dried black beans
12 cups (3 qt/3 l) cold water
1 ham bone or hock or prosciutto bone
3 tablespoons olive oil
3 large onions, diced, about 6 cups (1½ lb/750 g)
8 cloves garlic, minced
1½ teaspoons ground cinnamon
½ teaspoon ground cloves
1 teaspoon ground cumin
2 teaspoons dry mustard dissolved in 1 tablespoon sherry vinegar
2 tablespoons grated orange zest
½ cup (4 fl oz/125 ml) dark rum
1 cup (8 fl oz/250 ml) fresh orange juice
salt and freshly ground pepper to taste
sour cream, optional
thin slices of orange, optional

*P*ick over the beans to remove any debris. Soak the beans overnight in water to cover amply. Drain. Place the beans in a large pot, add the cold water and the hock or bone and bring to a boil. Reduce the heat to a simmer.

❧ In a large sauté pan, heat the olive oil. Add the onions and cook until tender, about 10 minutes. Add the garlic, cinnamon, cloves, cumin, mustard mixed with vinegar, and orange zest and cook 2 more minutes. Add this mixture to the beans. Cook, partially covered, until the beans are very ten-

bone or ham hock and discard. Purée the soup in batches in a blender or a food processor. If desired, cool, cover and refrigerate for up to 1 day.

❧ Return the soup to the heat and bring to a boil. Stir in the rum and orange juice. Season well with salt and pepper. Ladle into bowls and garnish each serving with sour cream and a thin slice of orange, if desired.

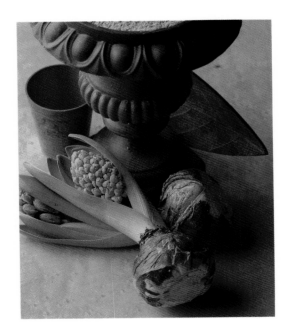

*P*lan on potting flowering bulbs in a large urn or stoneware vase early in the season so they'll be in full bloom on New Year's Day.

Quesadillas; Black Bean Soup with Dark Rum & Orange Zest

CHOCOLATE POUND CAKE

MAKES ONE 9- BY 5- BY 3-INCH
(23- BY 13- BY 7.5-CM) CAKE

*Dust the pound cake with powdered sugar
if you wish. To serve, slice it to be eaten
by hand, or serve on plates topped with
whipped cream or ice cream.*

1½ cups (6 oz/185 g) sifted all-purpose
 (plain) flour
½ cup (2 oz/60 g) sifted unsweetened
 Dutch-process cocoa
¼ teaspoon salt
2 oz (60 g) bittersweet chocolate
1 cup (8 oz/250 g) unsalted butter at
 room temperature
2 cups (14 oz/440g) light brown
 sugar, packed
3 eggs
1 teaspoon vanilla extract (essence)
1 cup (8 oz/250 g) sour cream

𝒫reheat an oven to 350°F (180°C).
Butter a 9- by 5- by 3-inch (23- by
13- by 7.5-cm) loaf pan. Sift the flour,
cocoa and salt together. Set aside. Place
the chocolate in the top of a double
boiler and melt over simmering water.
❧ In a large bowl, beat the butter and
brown sugar together until fluffy. Beat
in the eggs, one at a time. Add the
vanilla and the melted chocolate and
mix well. Fold a third of the dry ingredients, then half the sour cream into the
chocolate mixture; repeat, ending with
the dry ingredients. Pour the batter into
the prepared loaf pan.
❧ Bake until a toothpick inserted in
the center of the cake comes out clean,
about 1 hour. If the cake is browning
too quickly, cover it loosely with
aluminum foil. Let the cake cool in the
pan on a rack for 10 minutes, then turn
out onto the rack to cool completely.
Slice and serve.

*𝒜rrange personal collectibles with
tropical or regular greenery on a side
table for an eye-catching decoration.*

Chocolate Pound Cake

FESTIVE OCCASIONS

| BASIC RECIPES | AÏOLI | BEEF STOCK |

FESTIVE OCCASIONS

| BAGUETTES | COUNTRY BREAD | |
| MAKES THREE 1-LB (500-G) LOAVES | MAKES TWO 1¾-LB (875-G) LOAVES | |

1–2 days longer to develop the flavor.
To make the bread, place the yeast and
the starter with the warm water in the bowl

FESTIVE OCCASIONS

ROASTING & CARVING

Golden brown on the outside, moist and tender within, whole roast poultry, prime rib of beef, or leg of lamb makes a magnificent main course for any festive dinner party. The guidelines below will help you achieve the best results whenever you prepare one of these roasts.

Cooking times will vary with the size of the roast and, for red meats, the degree of doneness you desire. Bear in mind, too, that roasts put into the oven straight from the refrigerator will take longer to cook, so it's best to let the meat stand at room temperature for about 1 hour before roasting. Be sure you allow enough time to cook the roast and let it stand before carving so that dinner is not delayed.

To check the roast for doneness, use a meat thermometer; the instant-read kind is accurate and easy to use. After cooking, let roasts rest at room temperature, loosely covered with aluminum foil, for about 15 minutes before carving. This lets the meat reabsorb its juices and makes it moist and tender. The meat also continues to cook, adding 5°–7°F (2°–3°C) to the final temperature.

Roasting Turkey

Preheat an oven to 350°F (180°C). Place the turkey breast-side down on a rack in a roasting pan and tent it loosely with aluminum foil.

Place the turkey in the oven and roast, turning it breast-side up for the last 45 minutes of cooking, until it is golden brown all over and an instant-read thermometer inserted into the thickest part of the thigh, not touching the bone, registers 180°F (82°C). For an 8–12-lb (4–6-kg) turkey, total roasting time will be 2–3¼ hours. For a 12–16-lb (6–8-kg) turkey, 3¼–4¼ hours. For a 16–20-lb (8–10-kg) turkey, 4¼–5 hours.

For a stuffed turkey, add 30–45 minutes to the total roasting time.

Roasting Chicken

Preheat an oven to 325°F (165°C). Place the chicken on its side on a rack in a roasting pan.

Roast the chicken until it is golden brown, turning it on the other side, and then finishing it breast-side up, at even intervals during cooking.

Remove the chicken from the oven when an instant-read thermometer inserted into the thickest part of the thigh, not touching the bone, registers 180°F (82°C). For a 2–4-lb (1–2-kg) chicken, total roasting time will be 1–1½ hours. For a 4–7-lb (2–3.5-kg) chicken, 1½–2 hours.

Roasting Prime Rib of Beef

Preheat an oven to 500°F (260°C). Place the prime rib roast rib-side down in a roasting pan and roast it for 15 minutes.

Reduce the heat to 325°F (165°C) and continue roasting until the meat is browned and reaches the desired degree of doneness.

For rare beef, remove the roast when an instant-read thermometer inserted into the center of the meat, not touching the bone, registers 120°F (50°C), about 15 minutes per pound (500 g). For medium beef, remove when an instant-read thermometer registers 135°F (57°C), about 20 minutes per pound (500 g).

Roasting Leg of Lamb

Preheat an oven to 350°F (180°C). Place the lamb on a rack in a roasting pan and roast in the oven until it is browned and cooked to the desired doneness.

For rare to medium-rare lamb, remove when an instant-read thermometer inserted into the thickest part, not touching the bone, registers 135°–140°F (57°–60°C) about 1½ hours for a 6–7-lb (3–3.5-kg) leg.

For medium lamb, remove when an instant-read thermometer inserted into the thickest part, not touching the bone, registers 150°F (65°C), about 2 hours.

CARVING TURKEY

Carve only as much dark leg meat and white breast meat as you need to serve at one time, completing one side of the turkey before starting the next. Use a slicing knife with a long, flexible, but sturdy blade.

1. Remove the leg and the wing.
Cut through the skin between the leg and breast to locate the thigh joint; cut through the joint to sever the leg. To remove the wing (shown at left), cut through the shoulder joint where it meets the breast.

2. Slice the drumstick and thigh.
Cut through the joint to separate the drumstick and thigh. Serve them whole or carve them, cutting the meat into thin slices parallel to the bone.

3. Carve the breast.
Just above the thigh and shoulder joints, carve a deep horizontal cut toward the bone to create a base cut. Starting near the breastbone, carve thin slices vertically, cutting parallel to the rib cage and ending at the base cut.

CARVING CHICKEN

Carving a chicken is similar to carving a turkey. But because the bird is smaller, you may use a smaller knife, which is easier to handle. The breast can be removed in several slices, as for turkey, or in one piece.

1. Remove the leg and the wing.
Cut through the skin between the leg and breast to locate the thigh joint; cut through the joint to sever the leg (shown at left). Cut through the shoulder joint where it meets the breast to remove the wing.

2. Separate the drumstick and thigh.
If the chicken is small, serve the whole leg as one portion. If it is large, cut through the joint to separate the drumstick and thigh into two pieces.

3. Carve the breast.
Starting at the breastbone, cut downward and parallel to the rib cage, carving the meat into long, thin slices. Or, cut away the meat from the breastbone in one piece.

CARVING PRIME RIB OF BEEF

A prime rib is fairly simple to carve, provided you have a large, sharp knife for slicing and a sturdy fork to steady the roast. Serve some slices still attached to the ribs for guests who like the bones.

1. Cut the first slice.
Place the roast, ribs down, on a carving surface and steady it by inserting a carving fork into the top. Cut a vertical slice against the grain down to the rib bone; cut along the bone to free the slice.

2. Continue carving.
Cutting parallel to the first slice, continue to carve slices of the desired thickness. As individual bones are exposed, cut between them to remove them; or leave them attached to a slice for guests who request them.

CARVING LEG OF LAMB

Shaped like an irregular, elongated pear, a leg of lamb presents something of a challenge to the carver. The keys to successfully carving the leg lie in cutting parallel to the bone and providing guests with slices from both sides of the leg.

1. Slice the rounded side of the leg.
Grasp the end of the shank bone with a kitchen towel and tilt it slightly upward. Carve a slice from the rounded outer side of the leg at its widest point, cutting away from you and parallel to the bone.

2. Cut parallel slices.
Cutting parallel to the first slice, continue carving the meat in thin slices until you have cut enough to serve each guest a slice.

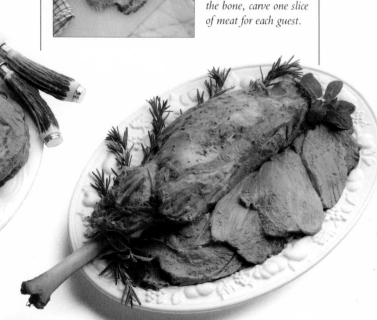

3. Carve the inner side of the leg.
Rotate the leg of lamb to expose its other, flatter side—the inner side of the leg, which is slightly more tender. Still cutting parallel to the bone, carve one slice of meat for each guest.

SETTING A TABLE

As the photographs on these pages illustrate, a wide array of specialized items is available for setting the dining table. The actual tableware you select, however, will vary with the menu, style and level of formality you desire. An informal setting (*below right*) draws on all-purpose, everyday pieces. A formal setting (*facing page*) employs more varied and elegant tableware.

❧ Whatever kind of table you set, some basic rules govern its arrangement. Plates, glasses, knives, forks and spoons are all placed in their accustomed spots with efficiency in mind, each set in the most convenient spot for your guests to use as the meal progresses.

Specialized glassware, distinguished by its shape, includes from left to right: white wineglass; rounded glass for Burgundy or other red wines; oversized balloon glass for red or white wine or water; all-purpose wineglass; snifter for Cognac or brandy; Champagne flute; sherry or dessert wineglass.

Additional flatware, that could supplement the standard pieces used in the place settings on these pages, includes from left to right: luncheon fork; luncheon knife; fish fork; fish knife, which also may be used for butter service; round-bowl spoon for cream soups; oval-bowl spoon for other soups; serving fork; serving spoon; slicer/server for appetizers, main courses or desserts.

❧ Logic lies behind the rules of serving and clearing at informal and formal tables alike. Food is always passed or served to each guest's left-hand side and cleared from the right. While the directions themselves are set in tradition, what matters most is the consistency that these rules bestow, literally keeping the meal's service flowing in a uniform direction.

INFORMAL SETTING

The setting shown below is informal in two basic ways. First, it uses everyday tableware, in this case, three pieces of stainless-steel flatware, a country-style pottery plate, a cotton napkin and an all-purpose glass.

❧ More significantly, the setting reflects the simplicity of the meal to come. A small fork awaits a first-course salad, to be followed by a main course for which the larger fork and the knife will be used. The single all-purpose glass indicates that one kind of wine, or perhaps water or some other nonalcoholic beverage, will be poured.

❧ Some general lessons for setting any informal table may be readily drawn from this basic arrangement. All implements are placed in the order in which they will be used. The napkin goes to the left of the plate and forks, its folded side facing the plate, ready to be picked up by a corner, opened and placed in the lap when a guest sits down. Next comes the first-course fork, then the dinner fork, closest to the plate.

❧ The dinner knife goes to the right of the plate, its blade facing inward, ready for the guest to pick it up for cutting. If soup were planned as a preliminary course, its spoon would be placed just to the right of the knife, since most people eat soup with their right hand. The glass is positioned above and just inside the knife, within easy reach but well clear of cutlery and plates.

❧ Other implements are notable by their absence. For an informal meal, dessert forks or spoons arrive at the table with that course, placed on the side of each plate. Likewise, teaspoons are offered only when coffee is passed, placed on the side of each saucer, thus avoiding unnecessary table clutter earlier in the meal.

❧ Whatever informal setting you arrange, you might also want to consider using place mats. They not only protect an attractive table, but also highlight each individual setting and add to the ambience with their color or pattern.

All-Purpose Glass

Napkin

Dinner Fork

Salad Fork

Dinner Plate

Dinner Knife

FORMAL SETTING

This setting reflects the more elegant style and the greater complexity of a formal meal. Fine china is complemented by silver flatware, an embroidered linen napkin and cut-crystal glasses with gold rims. As a backdrop for these fine accessories, a linen tablecloth could cover the table or, if the table's surface is beautiful in its own right, it could be left bare.

❧ Each item is carefully positioned in the order in which it will be used. The napkin, folded into a simple rectangle to highlight its monogram, is on the far left, ready to be unfolded and placed in the lap; a more elaborate fold such as one of those shown on pages 182–183 might be placed in the center of the dinner plate.

❧ To the right of the napkin go the forks, arranged left to right in their order of use. In most cases, the dinner fork is placed closest to the plate, although a salad fork might take that position if the menu calls for salad to be served after the main course, in the European fashion. Above the forks, a small plate awaits

bread, with an individual butter knife laid across the top rim with its handle pointing to the right, since most people will pick it up with their right hand.

❧ The dinner knife, as always, goes just to the right of the plate, its blade facing inward. A soup spoon to the right of the knife indicates that soup is part of the menu.

❧ Glassware should also be arranged in order of use. Traditionally, the glasses are placed in a linear fashion, but we've chosen a more contemporary arrangement that saves room on the table: Within closest reach of the right hand is a glass for the white wine that is usually poured with first courses. To its left, a larger glass awaits the red wine that would be poured next. Above both glasses goes an even larger goblet for guests who might request water.

❧ In a formal setting such as this, dessert utensils may be placed on the table before the meal, just above the dinner plate. Logic, again, determines their exact positioning: The dessert spoon's handle faces right, since most guests are likely to pick it

up with their right hand, and the fork's handle points to the left, to be picked up easily with the left hand. Alternatively, the utensils could be placed on the sides of the dessert plates when they are served.

❧ Depending on your own formal menu, you can further elaborate the setting. Many different shapes and sizes of glasses and more than two dozen kinds of table utensils have evolved over the centuries; some of the most common appear in the box on the opposite page. But while their combination of elegance and functionality is appealing, such specialized items are not absolutely essential to a formal menu. Any table set with simplicity, order and, above all, a regard for the convenience and comfort of your guests will be elegant.

Water Goblet

Red Wineglass

Dessert Spoon

Bread Plate

Dessert Fork

White Wineglass

Dinner Fork

Dinner Knife

Salad Fork

Soup Spoon

Napkin

Dinner Plate

NAPKIN FOLDING

A napkin folded into one of the five simple, classic patterns shown here can add variety and style to any party table.

❧ We recommend using sturdy-weave cotton or linen, which is more absorbent and soil-resistant than synthetic or coated fabrics. For the crispest folds, iron the napkins first; you may also want to apply a light spray starch. A final decorative touch such as ribbon, twine, string or flowers adds extra charm.

❧ For clarity, the illustrations here use a plain 20-inch-square (50-cm) linen napkin. But feel free to choose any fabric, color, pattern and size that suits the setting and mood of your party.

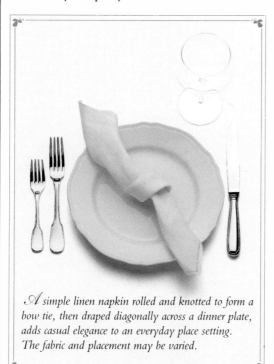

A simple linen napkin rolled and knotted to form a bow tie, then draped diagonally across a dinner plate, adds casual elegance to an everyday place setting. The fabric and placement may be varied.

BOW TIE

This easiest of folds has universal appeal, appearing in many of the menus in this book. As effortless in effect as it is quickly achieved, the bow tie works well with napkins of any fabric or size. This fold is ideal with a casual setting or even on a semi-formal table.

❧ For a striking effect, use this fold for such unconventional napkins as Western-style bandanas or large swatches of Indian madras cotton. You may also want to tuck little gifts inside the knots, such as the miniature rolling pins shown in the Indian Summer Brunch on page 74, to add an amusing touch that carries out the theme or ambience of your party.

1. Fold the upper left corner of the napkin to the lower right corner, forming a triangle.

2. Rotate so the tip faces you. Roll up from the bottom to form a cylinder.

3. Tie a knot in the center. Adjust the ends and knot to form a V shape or drape diagonally across a plate.

ASTORIA

The simple Astoria fold achieves a graceful effect suitable for both informal and elegant settings. For an attractive variation, omit folding down the top point in Step 2 to make a napkin with points at both ends.

1. Fold the napkin into quarters by first folding down the top half, then folding the left side over the right.

2. Rotate 90 degrees so the open end points toward you. Fold the top point down to the center.

3. Fold in the left corner so its point reaches just past the center.

4. Cross the right corner just over the left and carefully turn the napkin over.

BISHOP'S HAT

The bishop's hat has adorned fine tables for centuries and lends distinction to today's more formal occasions. You can present it either standing up or lying flat.

1. *Fold the upper left corner down to the lower right to form a triangle. Rotate so the long side faces you.*

2. *Holding your finger at the center of the long side, fold the right corner up to the top corner; then fold the left corner up to the top corner.*

3. *Fold the bottom corner up to within 1 inch (2.5 cm) of the top corner; then fold the bottom corner back down to touch the bottom edge.*

4. *Carefully turn the napkin over and fold the left side into the center.*

5. *Fold the right side into the center, tucking its point into the previous fold. Turn the napkin over again.*

BUFFET SERVER

Both attractive and useful, this fold yields a decorative napkin that conveniently holds an individual set of flatware for guests helping themselves to food. The buffet server also adds a creative touch when placed at an individual setting.

1. *Fold the napkin into quarters, rotating it so the open points are at the top.*

2. *Fold the point of the topmost layer down to meet the bottom corner, forming a pocket.*

3. *Fold the left and right corners underneath. Tuck cutlery inside the pocket.*

THE FAN

One of the most spectacular of napkin folds, the fan really dresses up a festive table such as the one set for the Heritage Christmas menu (*see page 145*). To make the napkin stand up stiffly, iron the pleats.

1. *Fold the napkin in half vertically to form a rectangle.*

2. *Starting at the bottom, fold back and forth into ½-inch (12-mm) accordion pleats, stopping when the unfolded portion is half as tall as it is wide.*

3. *Fold the napkin in half with the pleats on the outside.*

4. *Fold all the layers of the top square in half diagonally, tucking the point under the pleats. Lift the napkin from the right side so it stands up and the pleats fan out.*

FLOWER ARRANGING

Examples of casual, easily achieved flower arrangements may be found in almost every menu section of this book. For some festive occasions, you may want elaborate decorations of the kind you might order from a professional florist, but here we present three arrangements that can be done at home with lovely results. All that's required is a little time, imagination and patience, as well as the assistance of simple tools and materials available at a variety store, florist's supplier or hardware store.

Basic flower-arranging equipment (clockwise from top left): **1. florist's tape**, *for wrapping fragile stems, binding flowers together and strapping down florist's foam;* **2. florist's foam**, *or oasis, to be cut to fit into a bowl, soaked in water and used as a base into which flower stems are pushed;* **3. frogs**, *spiked metal disks into which stem or branch ends may be pushed to secure them;* **4. chicken wire**, *available in hardware stores, for use inside a bowl as a mesh to support branches and stems;* **5. clippers**, *to cut thicker stems or branches;* **6. shears**, *for cutting flower stems;* **7. gardening gloves**, *for handling thorny or prickly flowers;* **8. florist's wire**, *ranging from thin to thick gauges, for reinforcing stems or binding them together.*

FESTIVE ARRANGEMENT

Equally at home as a centerpiece or on a side table, this all-purpose arrangement may be created with a wide variety of flowers and greens. For the version shown here, we selected an array of white blossoms and delicate greenery: tulips, hyacinths, lilies of the valley, snowballs and ferns. You could

1. Secure the florist's foam in place in the container with strips of florist's tape.

3. Fill in the gaps by irregularly distributing more expensive blooms (here, snowballs and hyacinths). Finish with delicate flowers such as lilies of the valley.

vary the elements with your own favorite flowers in any pleasing combination, defining the overall shape with sturdier and less expensive blossoms and filling in with more delicate or costly blooms.

To prepare this arrangement, you will need a container with a wide mouth and low base; a chunk of florist's foam cut to fit the container; and florist's tape. At your flower shop, select eight to ten green fronds; about two dozen sturdy blossoms; and about a dozen each of two or more kinds of more delicate flowers. Use flower shears to cut all stems diagonally and put the flowers in warm water until ready to use; soak the foam in warm water for 30 minutes.

2. Create a fringe of ferns, inserting the stems around the base of the foam. Evenly insert less expensive, sturdy-stemmed flowers (we used tulips).

ROSE BRAID

A special occasion becomes even more memorable when decorated with roses. To give even more elegance to a rose bouquet, you could add a braid that cascades down the side of the vase.

❧ You'll need about four dozen roses in all. Depending on the style of your party, choose either a mix of colors or blossoms of a single hue. The loose, open petals of garden roses gives a more luxuriant look to the bouquet and braid; if you plan to use hot-house roses, buy them two days ahead of time so they can unfurl a bit. An urn-shaped vase will complement the elegance of the bouquet and provide height to lift the braid. Cut a piece of florist's foam to fit the container and presoak it in warm water for 30 minutes; place it inside the vase and add water. Arrange about three dozen of the roses, ends trimmed, in a bouquet shape and fill in any gaps with small roses or tight buds.

❧ To prepare the braid, select about 15 roses, in an even range of blossom sizes from small to large. Trim all their stems to a uniform 6-inch (15-cm) length. Place the roses in warm water until ready to use. As a base for the braid, use two 18-inch-long (45-cm) strips of variegated ivy, which has small, delicate leaves that contrast nicely with roses. If you like, you could make the braid longer, buying about a dozen more roses for each additional foot in length. Have on hand both florist's tape and thin florist's wire to secure the arrangement.

1. Hold the two 18-inch-long (45-cm) strands of ivy parallel to one another. At one end, attach three small partially opened roses with 6-inch (15-cm) stems, wrapping florist's wire around the stems and ivy. Trim the rose stems to 1 inch (2.5 cm) past the wire.

2. Continue attaching bunches of three roses, using the blossoms to conceal the wire of the previous bunch. Use fuller roses as you progress from beginning to end. Leave 5 inches (12.5 cm) of ivy bare at the end.

3. Tuck the ends of the bare ivy into the vase, sticking it into the florist's foam, and secure the braid inside and along the rim with florist's tape.

HOLIDAY TREE

Other attractive objects besides flowers make excellent candidates for festive arrangements. This centerpiece presents a tree-shaped composition of vegetables and fruits—an arrangement similar to the fruit tree in the Christmas dinner on page 147. You can give your imagination free rein when planning a holiday tree's elements, selecting from a wide range of foods and other materials and opting for either a monochromatic or varied color scheme.

❧ A 12-inch (30-cm) Styrofoam cone serves as the base for the tree, with wooden toothpicks used as fasteners. Because foods arranged in this way will not keep long, assemble the tree the day of the party.

1. Insert wooden toothpicks into the largest items (here, limes, Brussels sprouts and baby artichokes) and attach them to the base of the cone in several layers.

2. Fill the gaps with smaller items, such as broccoli, skewering them on toothpicks or, in the case of stringbeans, inserting them directly into the foam.

3. Top the tree with an attractive object (here, a small artichoke). Add final decorations (here, whole jalapeño chilies) by skewering them onto toothpicks so that they rest atop the other items.

and also is sold in powdered form. Look for products labeled *pure saffron*. Saffron threads have more flavor and should be crushed before use: First, put them in a metal kitchen spoon and hold the spoon over a hot burner

in a mortar with a pestle.

SHERRY
Fortified, cask-aged wine, ranging from dry to sweet, enjoyed as an aperitif and used as a flavoring in both savory and sweet recipes.

sharp-edged holes across the fruit's skin to remove the zest in thin strips, or by using the fine holes on a hand-held grater. Alternatively, remove strips of zest with a vegetable peeler, taking care not to remove any white pith. Thinly slice the strips with a small, sharp knife.

LOBSTER
Although many seafood stores and some food markets sell lobsters already cooked, cleaned and shelled, it is usually far more

Chanterelles (shown below), subtly flavored, pale yellow, trumpet-shaped wild mushrooms about 2–3 inches (5–7.5 cm) in length, are also cultivated commercially, and may be found in specialty-food markets and fruit and

for a milder flavor. Walnut oil has a rich, nutty taste prized in dressings; that made from toasted nuts has the deepest color and fullest flavor.

OLIVES

INDEX